A FINE TIME AT
MONKEY
ISLAND
...BLVD.—JUST OVER THE PASS
...OOD, CALIF.

A NEW STAND OF LIFE

THE WONDER SPOT
LAKE DELTON
AT
WISCONSIN DELLS

WILLEY HOUSE
CRAWFORD NOTCH, N.H.
WILD LIFE EXHIBIT

D0118679

JEROME'S TEPEE
ON
HIGHWAY 30
GRAND ISLAND
NEBRASKA

ED. CLARK'S
ESKIMO SLED
DOG RANCH
NORTH WOODSTOCK, N.H.

MONKEY
JUNGLE
22 MILES SOUTH OF MIAMI, FLA.

JOHN MARGOLIES

FUN ALONG THE ROAD

AMERICAN TOURIST ATTRACTIONS

A BULFINCH PRESS BOOK

LITTLE, BROWN AND COMPANY

BOSTON · NEW YORK · TORONTO · LONDON

CONTENTS

Chapter 1
AMAZING! INCREDIBLE! 6
SIGNS • STATUES • TALL PAUL

Chapter 2
FRAMING THE VIEW 30

Chapter 3
ONCE UPON A TIME 34
LET'S PRETEND • HO! HO! HO!
GHOST TOWNS • SMALLER THAN LIFE

Chapter 4
ZOO PARADE 58
IT'S FOR THE BIRDS • KING OF THE BEASTS • THE BEAR FACTS
MONKEY BUSINESS • FLIPPER'S FRIENDS
REPTILES GALORE • DINOSAURS

Chapter 5
MADE BY HAND 88

Chapter 6
PUTTERING AROUND 98

Chapter 7
GIFT SHOPS 108
SOUVENIRS

Chapter 8
ELEGY 120

ACKNOWLEDGMENTS 123
SOURCE CREDITS 123
BIBLIOGRAPHY 124

CHAPTER 1

AMAZING! INCREDIBLE!

Opposite: Although seemingly hundreds of billboards flash by before the Wall Drug exit off the interstate, nothing quite prepares visitors for the enormity and message-directed splendor of Wall Drug's animated billboard in Wall, South Dakota.

Below: Roadside bear cubs pulled them into a gas station in Belleville, Kansas.

When Americans first took to the road behind the wheels of their cars in the beginning of the twentieth century, a new set of facilities had to be invented to serve these happy wanderers. Shrewd entrepreneurs realized that the automotive nomads passing in front of their properties were a source of potential income, and very early on American ingenuity and the free enterprise system took hold at curbside. The most essential services for tourists were gas, food, and lodging: garages and blacksmith shops became gas stations; eating and drinking establishments, from the sublime to the mundane, popped up to satiate nearly every taste; and tents and campgrounds evolved into motels.

But in this explosion of commerce beside the road, there was a fourth type of establishment that had nothing whatsoever to do with fulfilling basic needs. The tourist attraction, in an almost infinite variety of manifestations, was conceived as a way to divert and amuse travelers along the way. The beginnings of the phenomenon are shrouded in the mists of the past, and just where and when these businesses began to appear is at best a matter of conjecture.

As one drove along almost any road in the early years, some form of roadside amusement would inevitably appear. It might be there one year and gone the next, only to be replaced by another attraction just a few miles away. Because of the *ad hoc* and nonsequential nature of roadside attractions, a straightforward and chronological explanation of their development is an impossible task. To present a panorama of this phenomenon, this book will highlight examples of a wide variety of roadside attractions, each with its own chronological development and special history. An overview of the entire genre, therefore, can be gleaned by considering the totality of these histories of some of the most significant, bizarre and typical examples.

One theory about how tourist attractions began is that people involved in serving up essentials added "amusement" facilities as a means of attracting attention and income, and to distinguish themselves from their competitors. In the 1920s a menagerie was added to Young's Rainbow Garden Tourist Cottage Camp in Council Grove, Kansas; two bear cubs were staked out and caged in front of a gas station in Belleville, Kansas; and at another auto camp near Macon, Georgia, there was a small zoo that featured a large black bear trained to guzzle bottles of soda pop provided by spectators.

Right: Prohibition Sally guzzled soda pop at Point Lookout, near Old Fort, North Carolina.

Below: Everything and monkeys, too, at Gallaway's Café in Falfurrias, Texas.

GALLAWAY'S, FALFURRIAS, TEX.

Because roadside attractions were hardly a necessity, the people who built them had to scream all the louder to attract customers. Intriguing and sometimes mysterious messages appeared on billboards throughout the United States to forewarn and seduce automotive explorers. Based upon the business histories of some major American attractions—places like Rock City, South of the Border, and Wall Drug—the key to their success has been the sheer number of billboards set out for the tourist to see and ponder.

The architectural expression of early roadside attractions ranged from the extravagant and outrageous to the deliberately bland. Programmatic buildings shaped as sculptural renditions of what was being offered—like a huge alligator or an orange—or enormous statues and entrance signs, made some roadside amusement facilities very hard to miss. Other attractions used the opposite approach. After miles and miles of billboards, they presented only a tall and otherwise featureless blockade by the side of the road. The curious tourists would have to stop, go inside, and pay an admission charge to see just what they'd been tempted by for miles and miles.

These "unnecessary" places also fulfilled needs as temporary way stations to stretch and relax, and they also provided very necessary rest rooms. Nearly always the bathrooms were made accessible even to those tourists not paying admission. But in order to get to them, the tourist would have to venture deep into the gift shops (which were also the final features on the tour of paying customers) through a maze of aisles chock-full of souvenirs, candy, and other assorted doodads.

Top: The end of the trail at Santa Claus, Arizona (north of Kingman).

Left: A gingerbread man fence at The Enchanted Forest, Ellicott City, Maryland, was a well-considered and decorative alternative to the often-encountered blank-wall facades.

"SPOT CARTER," OFFICIAL MASCOT OF ROCK CITY GARDENS, LOOKOUT MOUNTAIN

CASTLE of the GNOMES

CASTLE OF THE GNOMES IN FAIRYLAND CAVERNS, ROCK CITY GARDENS, LOOKOUT MOUNTAIN

Garnet Carter, an early roadside entrepreneur, came to own one of the great scenic overlooks in the United States when he and a partner purchased property on Lookout Mountain in Georgia near Chattanooga, Tennessee, in 1924. Mr. Carter and his wife, Frieda, a designer interested in horticulture, developed the ten acres atop the mountain, which became known as Rock City Gardens when it was opened to the public in 1932. At Rock City were paths meandering through gardens of specimen plants, and culminating in a scenic overlook called Lover's Leap from which one could marvel at an awesome view of seven states. To get to Lover's Leap, visitors can still walk across a solid rock bridge, or they can walk on the wild side and try the "swing along" suspension bridge across the abyss. Like other depression-era operations, business was not good at first. But then Garnet Carter

came up with the slogan "See Rock City" and an idea: to proclaim this message on painted barns. The number of Rock City barns proliferated, and so did the tourists. At one time Rock City maintained over 900 barns in the eastern United States. Now, fewer than 100 remain.

Down the road from Rock City is Ruby Falls, with two caves, one with a remarkable underground waterfall that Leo Lambert, the owner, named in honor of his wife, Ruby. In 1928 Lambert had an elevator shaft drilled through rock to shuttle tourists to the wondrous world below. The leftover limestone quarried from the shaft was used to construct a three-story-high observation tower above the cave, providing a panoramic view down upon the city of Chattanooga—the view in the opposite direction from Lover's Leap.

Left: In the 1920s "Spot Carter" was a beloved pet of Garnet and Frieda Carter, the developer-designers of Rock City on Lookout Mountain, Georgia (near Chattanooga, Tennessee), and the inventors, as well, of the Tom Thumb Golf chain.

Above: Fairyland Caverns at Rock City aren't caves at all; they were created in 1946. The "caverns" are a man-made tunnel through a cave-like crevice on the surface of Lookout Mountain. Along the passageway, a series of tableaux of gnomedom were built to appeal to younger visitors.

In other instances, ordinary businesses mutated into operations that overwhelmed their original functions. C. M. "Dad" Lee, a shrewd operator, became known as the "King of the Desert" when he operated a Shell gas station along the Victory Highway in Oreana, Nevada. "Dad," as he was always called, claimed to be a relative of Robert E. Lee, and he sported a goatee and tall brimmed hat. But there was much more than gas at Dad Lee's gas station. He assembled a group of rescued old buildings along the road in the 1920s and called them Lee Center, and he stocked them with a collection of Nevada relics and curios. And in his obituary in a local paper in 1934, we learn that Dad Lee was a bootlegger as well: "It was also a matter of considerable satisfaction to many thirsty travelers to discover, upon visiting 'Dad,' that gas and water were not all that was sold in the curio shop."

Top: Ruby Falls observation tower, a National Register "Irish Castle" with a view of Chattanooga, Tennessee, from its tower lookout, is located atop cave formations, with the Ruby Falls in one of the caves. The excavated elevator shafts were the source of the limestone used on the facade of the building.

Right: Dad Lee, the "King of the Desert" along Highway 40 near Winnemucca, Nevada, had curios, "historic" buildings full of old stuff, souvenirs, gas, and eats. He was also said to have done a land-office business in bootleg liquor.

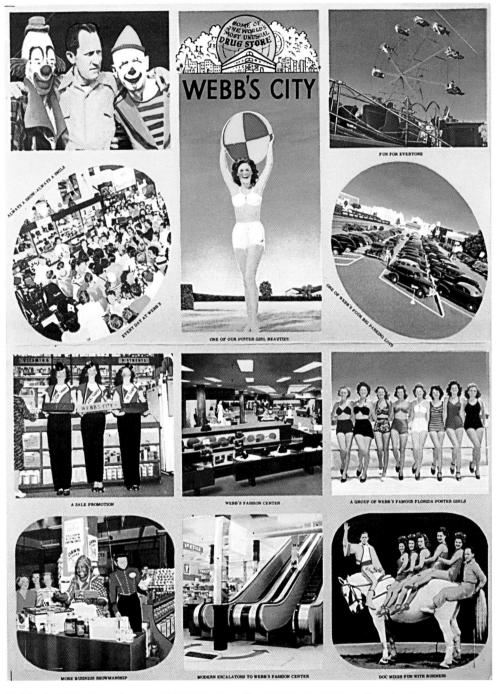

ONE OF OUR POSTER GIRL BEAUTIES

FUN FOR EVERYONE

ONE OF WEBB'S FOUR BIG PARKING LOTS

A SALE PROMOTION

WEBB'S FASHION CENTER

A GROUP OF WEBB'S FAMOUS FLORIDA POSTER GIRLS

MORE BUSINESS SHOWMANSHIP

MODERN ESCALATORS TO WEBB'S FASHION CENTER

DOC MIXES FUN WITH BUSINESS

Webb's Cut Rate Drugs became Webb's City from the 1920s to the 1970s as it evolved into a complex of 72 stores on ten blocks of downtown St. Petersburg, Florida. The merchandising hysteria and marketing genius were provided by Doc Webb himself, a man who got his start at medicine shows in the hills of Tennessee before greatly enlarging the scope of his operations.

James Earl "Doc" Webb was another early businessman who transformed a once humble business into what was literally almost a "three-ring circus." Webb opened his original drugstore in St. Petersburg, Florida, in 1925 with a 3-foot counter in a 17-by-25-foot space. He went on to develop a retailing empire called Webb's City, the "World's Most Unusual Drug Store," with seven buildings covering ten blocks of downtown St. Petersburg. Doc Webb could be found in and about his stores wearing one of his 150 custom-made suits with matching silk ties, and he would shout special prices into a microphone. In addition, he offered such other thrills as circus acts in the parking lot, in which Webb sometimes put in a guest appearance, shows featuring a chorus line of Webb's famous Florida poster girls, or a man milking a rattlesnake.

It's hard to imagine that the same type of thing could have happened to more than one drugstore. But it began to happen again in 1931 when Ted Hustead bought a 24-by-60-foot building containing a patent medicine store and soda fountain on the Main Street of Wall, South Dakota, for $3,000. This coincided with the depths of the depression, and not surprisingly, business was not good at the beginning. But in 1936, Ted's wife, Dorothy, inspired by some Burma Shave signs she had seen, thought

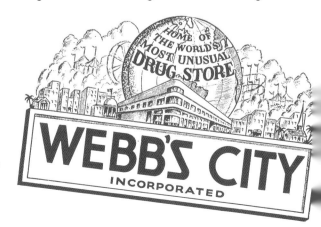

12

Left: Wall Drug's first and most famous promotion in the 1930s offered tourists "Free Ice Water" on a Burma Shave–like series of billboards on the edge of town. But before long, the willing visitors were also exposed to the temptations of Ted Hustead's soda fountain.

Bottom: Once upon a time in 1931, Ted Hustead bought a little drugstore on the Main Street of Wall, South Dakota. No one could have predicted that it would evolve into a tourist attraction of international fame and nearly boundless proportions, some 60,000 square feet of it.

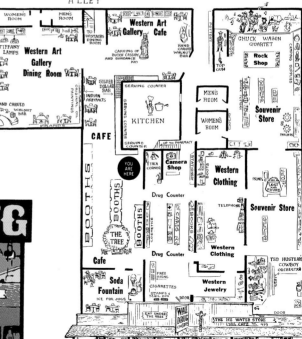

that it would be a good idea to put up a series of signs on nearby Route 16A to attract tourists to the store: "Get a soda / Get root beer / Turn next corner / Just as near / To Highway 16 And 14 / Free Ice Water / Wall Drug." The signs helped business, and as they proliferated nearly endlessly, so did the number of customers. Wall Drug, in this town of 800 people, became a huge complex of stores—60,000 square feet, with the main building 149 by 249 feet—drawing 10,000 visitors or more a day during the summer season to see life-size, carved wooden statues of historical personages, groups of animated figures such as the Cowboy Orchestra, photographic exhibitions, a western clothing store, a pharmacy museum, a rock shop, oodles of souvenirs, of course, a travelers chapel, and even prescriptions for medicine in this the only drugstore within a 6,000-square-mile area. Now over sixty years old, Wall Drug is an American institution run by Ted's son Bill, and two of his grandsons. And even Ted himself still comes into work three days a week.

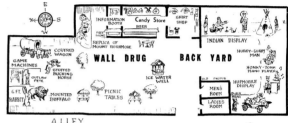

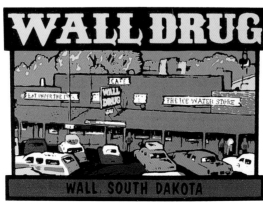

FUN ALONG THE ROAD

Above right: Highway puns prevail for miles and miles on all sides of South of the Border, a roadside extravaganza just south of the North Carolina border in Dillon, South Carolina.

Right: At the top of the observation tower at South of the Border, one can catch a sombrero-focused panoramic view of the interstate highway just below it, as well as of the surrounding terrain. The attraction began as a beer stand–turned–restaurant, added a motel, and then it went crazy, covering some 350 acres by the highway: 14 gift shops, a miniature golf course—the Golf of Mexico—and nearly 100 wildly painted fiberglass animal statues scattered all about.

South of the Border in Dillon, South Carolina, a Mexican-theme attraction operated by Alan Schafer beside the interstate just south of the North Carolina border, is nearly as hectic as Wall Drug. It began in the 1950s as an 18-by-36-foot beer stand, and then a 10-seat grill was added. In 1964, a 20-unit a motel was built, and the whole works assumed its present identity as South of the Border. As part of the motel experience, Mexican (and later non-Mexican) boys all named "pedro" (with a generic small "p") showed surprised guests to their rooms by leading them there on bicycles. But perhaps better known than the attraction itself are its humorous and outrageous billboards. By now, there are over 250 billboard messages, full of puns and jokes, stretching along the eastern United States from Philadelphia to Daytona Beach, tempting people to stop and shop at a conglomeration of buildings spread across some 350 acres.

Many of the earliest attractions were begun in the friendly climates in the southernmost locations in the United States, particularly in the tourist-frenzied states of Florida and California where endless summer prevails. Alligator farms and ostrich farms were popular draws in the first decade of the twentieth century. In addition to allowing amazed tourists to ride on a saddle perched upon the backs of ostriches, or to see other brave souls wrestling alligators, these very same operations were also in the business of making and selling shoes, handbags, and feather boas. The Arkansas Alligator Farm and Petting Zoo in Hot Springs, Arkansas, founded in 1902, celebrates its early history by proclaiming that "in all probability

your Great Grandparents visited the farm. It is truly one of the oldest show places in Hot Springs."

Other zoos and animal attractions sprang up nearly everywhere. Perhaps the most fascinating of them all was the I.Q. Zoo in Hot Springs, Arkansas. It was founded by two expert animal psychologists,

Keller Breland (above) and his wife, Marian, turned their expertise into big business. They have supplied specially trained animals to institutions throughout the United States and beyond. They also operated the I.Q. Zoo in Hot Springs, Arkansas, so tourists could see first-hand the likes of Clara and Rufus busy at their appoined tasks.

Keller and Marian Breland, who based their work with animals upon B. F. Skinner's concept of "operant conditioning" (Mrs. Breland was Skinner's second graduate student at the University of Minnesota). They discovered that the best way to train most animals was to give them an immediate reward of food for a specific task that would be repeated over and over. Instead of remaining in their ivory tower, the Brelands decided in 1947 to open a commercial business, Animal Behavior Enterprises, based upon their expertise. The Brelands opted for a warmer climate and moved to a 260-acre farm outside Hot Springs in 1950, and Marian Breland (now Bailey) reports that "Finally, in 1955, somewhat in desperation, we opened the I.Q. Zoo in downtown Hot Springs to satisfy local curiosity and attract tourists seeking entertainment."

A visit to the I.Q. Zoo must have been a real treat. There, in a variety of entertaining and clever displays, some of which were coin-operated, could be found: Bert Backquack and his Barnyard Band; Chickey Mantle, the baseball-playing chicken; Romeo Rabbit, the kissing bunny; Priscilla Pig, who put large coins in a piggy bank; and many more animals performing astonishing feats. In addition, the Brelands designed shows for large corporations such as General Mills, and also provided training methods and show design to other animal attractions throughout the country, including Marineland of Florida with its great performing dolphins, Parrot Jungle in Miami, and Knott's Berry Farm in Buena Park, California. Keller Breland died in 1965, and his widow remarried and continued to operate the I.Q. Zoo until 1990.

An animal attraction of an entirely different sort can still be found in San Antonio, Texas. It is now called the Lone Star Buckhorn Museum, and since 1956 it has been installed adjacent to the Lone Star Brewery. This location is entirely appropriate because this institution began as the Buckhorn Saloon in 1881, the very same place immortalized by Larry McMurtry in *Lonesome Dove*. A man named Albert Friedrich, whose father made furniture from animal horns, began his own collection of animal horns as he opened the saloon. As the years went by and as the saloon prospered, he collected hundreds upon hundreds of sets of mounted horns and heads. During Prohibition the business became known as Albert's Curio Store and then the Buckhorn Curio Store and Café. As a souvenir shop, it sold a curious batch of products, including such items as armadillo baskets, abalone pearl manicure sets, postcards, horn chairs, and rattlesnake hatbands.

The Lone Star Buckhorn Museum in San Antonio, Texas, an institution that lives on to this day, began as the Longhorn Saloon in the late nineteenth century. Its owner, Albert Friedrich, was looking for unique decor, and then accumulated it in vast quantities. The prize mounted longhorn is "Old Tex" with horns spanning more than eight feet from tip to tip.

16

The collection is certainly extraordinary—horns and mounted animal heads from all over the world, with Texas and other North American species having the greatest representation. Perhaps the most outstanding examples are the Brady Buck, a seventy-eight-point deer head, and "the largest mass of horns in the world" from an African oxen with a twenty-one-inch diameter where the horns attach to the skull. Another mind-boggling part of the collection is a grouping of over 32,000 rattlesnake rattles, some of which were arranged by Mrs. Friedrich into "pictures" of such subjects as a life-size antlered deer and another depicting two Indian heads.

In Florida as in Texas, attractions continued to pop up nearly everywhere in the 1940s and 1950s, and not all of them were that entertaining or inspired. At least a few of them even put human beings on display. Some of these places, perhaps unintentionally, reinforced the ethnic and racial stereotyping prevalent in the 1940s and 1950s. Black people and especially Seminole Indians were exploited and used as the lure for many "exotic" attractions. An old brochure, probably from the 1940s, for Musa Isle, a small place in the heart of Miami, which boasted that it was the "home of the Seminole Indians," goes on to tell the tourists that: ". . . here you will see the 'Silent Seminoles' living and working in their own primitive way, making curios and novelties in their own crude and interesting way."

Top: A tourist group aboard a cruise on the *Seminole Queen* in 1943 stops off and poses in front of Musa Isle in Miami, Florida.

Right: A Seminole woman cranks out another souvenir at the Indian Village at Musa Isle.

M.148—Seminole Maid
Engaged in Native Handicraft at Musa Isle
Indian Village, Miami, Florida

Black Americans made out little better at Wakulla Springs, near Tallahassee. At Wakulla, a glass-bottom boat place, we are told about a black bass that jumped over a pole, Henry the Pole Vaulting Fish. "Seeing's Believing," claims the brochure, which then goes on to explain that "a great understanding grew between the Negro guides and Henry. Today Henry will not perform for anyone else."

But at the Lewis Plantation and Turpentine Still in Brooksville, Florida, Pearce Lewis latched on to a really bad idea and then went on to promote it to the tourist trade. This attraction showed, as described briefly in one brochure, "Plantation days just as they existed in pre-civil [sic] War and antebellum days. Turpentine is distilled, Negroes dance

A Trip Through The
Old Lewis Plantation
BROOKSVILLE
FLORIDA

LEWIS PLANTATION
and TURPENTINE STILL
The Untouched South

by
PEARCE LEWIS

TYPICAL NEGRO CASH AND SINGERS
LEWIS TURPENTINE STILL AND PLANTATIONS   BROOKSVILLE, FLORIDA
C-284

and sing in their natural environment." A more detailed brochure for the attraction itself elaborates that "in addition to an actual, hale and hearty ex-slave, some 200 happy descendants of former slaves" can be seen. "Pickaninnies are at play in the sand, . . . a carefree darky plaintively strums a guitar with a melody to his lady love," and "typical mammies are washing clothes in primitive black iron boilers. . . ."

Above and left: The Lewis Plantation and Turpentine Still in Brooksville, Florida, was more than a step behind the times. It showed, as a tourist attraction, life as it was presumed to be in the Old South when there was still slavery.

There was another genre of tourist attractions that were purposely designed to be incredible—the so-called Mystery Spots and Spook Hills. In these places, we are told that the laws of gravity are defied. People stand atilt at a pronounced angle, as numerous postcards show. Water runs up. Cars back up hills with their motors turned off. All very mysterious, and all very explainable. In the specially built mystery houses, the optical illusion of gravity gone berserk is achieved by slightly tilted floors within a closed environment with pictures hung at the same angle as the floors and similar tromp l'oeil feats of deception. Spook Hills are harder to explain in a few words, but they work on the same principle as the Mystery Spots within carefully chosen outdoor locations.

Finally, another carefully crafted form of tourist attraction, examples of so-called folk art constructed by dedicated and idiosyncratic artists, were often opened to visitors for an admission charge. Simon Rodia's Watts Towers in Los Angeles are the best-known example of this phenomenon. But there were many more, including Edward Leedskalnin's cosmic and ethereal Coral Castle (page 92) in Homestead, Florida, and Father Dobberstein's Grotto of Redemption (page 95) in West Bend, Iowa.

With the approach of the millennium, the standardization and sterilization wrought by the Interstate Highway System, and the growing sophistication of parents and children alike, one might surmise that these artifacts of the good old

Left: At Magnetic Hill in Moncton, New Brunswick, Canada (one of a number of strange inclines in various locales), visitors are astonished as their cars, with ignitions turned off, seem to defy gravity by backing up the hill.

Bottom: Everything was topsy-turvy at places like The Wonder Spot, in Lake Delton, Wisconsin (left), and "the famous" Miracle House in East Manitou Springs, Colorado.

days of tourism might have become an endangered species. But this is not the case. Yes, some of the smaller and funkier examples have fallen by the wayside as the people who built them beside now

bypassed highways have come and gone. But other attractions have thrived by making themselves bigger and "better." Some, which began as places where fairy tales came to life, have become huge amusement parks. Storytown U.S.A. in Lake George, New York, while retaining much of its early charm, has now become The Great Escape Fun Park with the addition of an enormous roller coaster and other elaborate and sophisticated thrill rides. And in Santa Claus, Indiana, the old Santa Claus Land attraction has now become known as the very "cool" Holiday World and Splashin' Safari.

Left: Agnes Jones was a black artist-entrepreneur in Lake City, Florida, about 1915 to 1920. Aunt Agnes, as she was called, had her sculptural objects made from animal bones, curios in the house, and "oceans of flowers in her garden."

Bottom left: Even literary heroes became souvenir bait at The Shop by the Side of the Road near Concord, Massachusetts.

Bottom right: In the old days, some tourist attractions weren't content to sit in one place beside the road. Hale's Traveling Museum out of Cheyenne, Wyoming, was a 1926 Nash chock full of relics and oddities, and it was ready to appear wherever crowds might be.

It is interesting to note that small theme parks like Storytown and Santa Claus Land were precursors to the new super theme park amusement industry, which began in Southern California on July 17, 1955, when Walt Disney opened Disneyland, where the thematic ideas of storybooks and Main Streets were combined with other spectacular rides and experiences based upon new technologies that were just then evolving.

Although the names, faces, and attractions themselves have changed, the basic idea and function of these tourist meccas remain the same. The people who have operated roadside amusements throughout the years are in the business of providing fun and entertainment. Roadside attractions are a popular American tradition of nearly unfathomable proportions; they have the same kind of appeal as sideshows at the circus. Often these facilities are targeted not only to the children riding in the backseats but also to the children living within the adults in the front seat as well. And so, life along the road, full of surprises and adventures, continues as American families keep on taking vacations in their cars, exploring the wonders, both scenic and man-made, in the far corners of the United States.

Lake City, Fla. Agnes Jones in the Boneyard.

SIGNS & STATUES

The very lifeblood of a roadside attraction is its means of proclaiming itself beside the road. In the old days, before the interstates, this process was much easier than it is today: set up your business and then strategically place a number of billboards in the line of traffic, increasing the number and the intensity of the messages as the irresistible what-ever comes closer. Sometimes these messages were conveyed by artfully rendered, hand-painted im-ages which, in and of themselves, were notable ex-amples of commercial folk art. Artful or not, these signs had to gain the attention of the passersby, especially the children riding along, anxious only to alleviate the boredom of a long trip and to see something that was "neat" and "cool."

The 38-foot-high fiberglass Uncle Sam statue from the Danbury (Connecticut) Fair was brought to the Magic Forest, Lake George, New York, in 1981 to serve as its roadside beacon on Route 9.

Fairfield, Pennsylvania.

Peach Water Tower, Gaffney, South Carolina.

Ute Indian Trading Post, Vernal, Utah.

Not only did businesses use oversized icons to achieve their objectives, but small towns throughout the United States have used this trick to help to create an immediately recognizable identity for themselves: an enormous peach-shaped water tower by an interstate in South Carolina exuberantly celebrates this important local crop; the world's largest buffalo, a gargantuan statue, can be found on the outskirts of Jamestown, North Dakota, to delight the passing parade; and a large Superman statue helps to define where else but Metropolis, Illinois.

Sevierville, Tennessee.

Statue for a water slide in Virginia Beach, Virginia.

Homestead, Florida.

World's Largest Pecan, James Pecan Shop, Brunswick, Missouri.

Spearfish, South Dakota.

TROUT HAVEN ½ MILLION CAUGHT

23

The Hogan Indian Arts and Crafts, Mancos, Colorado.

Big John, Bulcan Iron Mountain Iron Mine, Norway, Michigan.

Jolly Green Giant, Blue Earth, Minnesota.

Tawas City, Michigan.

Near Lake Delton, Wisconsin.

Chimney Rock, North Carolina.

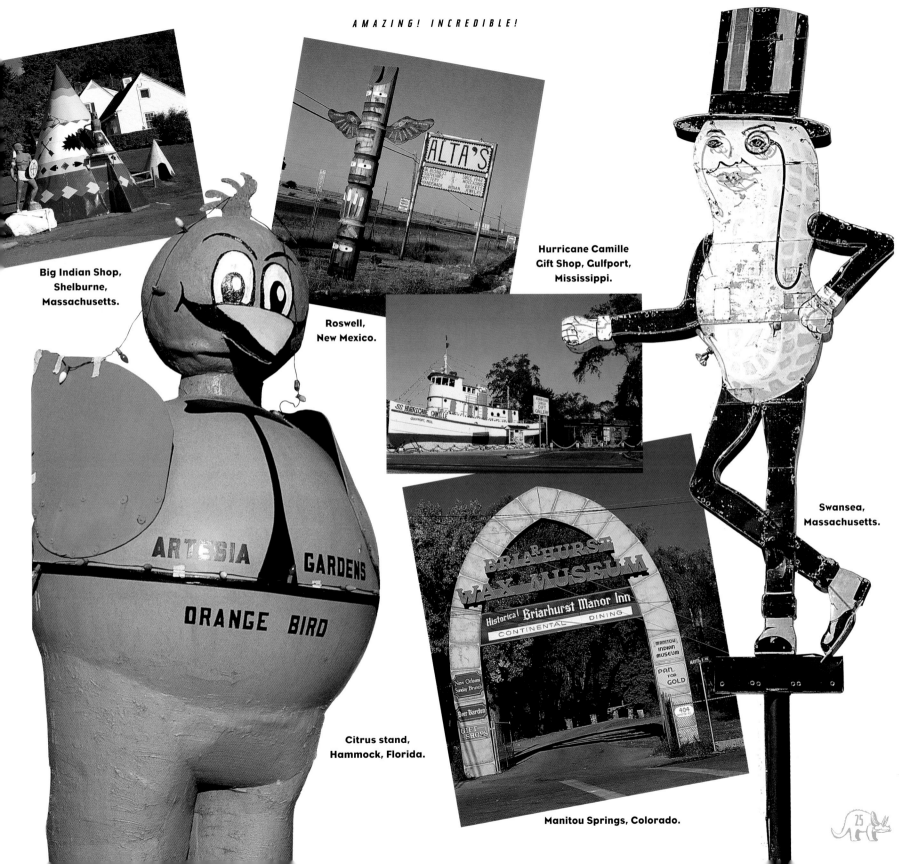

Big Indian Shop,
Shelburne,
Massachusetts.

Hurricane Camille
Gift Shop, Gulfport,
Mississippi.

Roswell,
New Mexico.

Swansea,
Massachusetts.

Citrus stand,
Hammock, Florida.

Manitou Springs, Colorado.

TALL PAUL

Paul Bunyan is one of the great folk legends of America. The exact origins of this giant woodsman and his famous blue ox, Babe, are unknown. But their cultural popularity is proven by an endless array of tall tales and folderol that embellish this legend. Since he is an oversized figure of our collective imaginations, tall Paul has become a perfect roadside commercial symbol. Huge apparitions of Paul Bunyan have been used to promote numerous businesses throughout the United States through the years. And since Paul is the epitome of fun and nonsense, he has become the silly symbol of choice for tourist attractions of many sorts.

BABE Paul Bunyons BLUE OX.

Trees of Mystery Entrance on Redwood Highway.

56/6-ART-RAY

Left: The dynamic duo at Weinke's Paul Bunyan Lookout, Spruce, Michigan, date from different eras: Babe was executed in 1938 by Paul Domke, master-builder of the dinosaur garden up the highway a few miles away. Paul was the creation of Walter Hayden in 1953-54.

Right: The classic Paul Bunyan and Babe in Bemidji, Minnesota, have been there doing their thing—attracting tourists—since the 1930s, and they are seen below right in a comic chrome postcard from the 1960s.

Below: The first Paul Bunyan and Babe statues at the Trees of Mystery along the Redwood Highway in Klamath, California, (dating from 1947), were placed wide apart. Huge new replacements now stand side-by-side.

RAN INTO PAUL BUNYAN WHILE TOURING MINNESOTA......

Lakewood's Paul Bunyan, Lakewood,
Wisconsin, is wearing real oversized clothing,
sure to have not withstood the stress of very
many winters. Paul's sweetheart, Lucette Diana
Kensack, stood 20 feet high in Hackensack,
Minnesota (and, we are told, the town was
named in her honor).

Scattered throughout the United States, but mainly in the upper Midwest and Northwest, are less than subtle reminders of the power and might of the legendary woodsman (clockwise from right): Paul's Pipe, location unknown; his Smelt Fryin' Pan in Escanaba, Michigan; one of his 10-foot-high boots at the Trees of Mystery in Klamath, California; his wheelbarrow in Lake Itaska, Minnesota; and his spoon, fork, and mug at Weinke's Paul Bunyan Lookout in Spruce, Michigan.

FRAMING THE VIEW

Tourists continue a tradition at Silver Springs, Florida, by gliding in a glass-bottom boat-observatory, invented here in 1878 when a man named Hullam Jones installed a glass viewing box in a dugout canoe. The object has always been to view marine life below, alive and well in the crystal clear spring waters.

A mong the earliest types of tourist attractions were especially beautiful spots in the natural environment itself, some with panoramic views of the landscape from above, and others through "windows" to see beneath the water. Entrepreneurs used a variety of methods to take what was already a given and then package it so that it could attract the maximum number of visitors. The most common and direct way to provide a specific view of the surrounding terrain was to build observation towers, and they loomed upward in a surprising array of architectural expressions. The tower attracts attention, and since a direct point of access is established, restaurants and gift shops can be located at its base.

Perhaps the most unusual observation towers in all of the United States are the nearly identical, 64-feet-high twin towers, built cheek-by-jowl atop a bluff in the Irish Hills of southeastern Michigan. How they came to happen is quite a tale in itself, conjuring up memories of the feuding Hatfields and

McCoys. It seems that the property line on this particular hill bisected the site. In the 1920s, the Michigan Observation Company (MOC) decided to build a tower to provide a view of some twenty lakes in the surrounding area. One side of the hill was owned by the Brighton family and the other by the Kelly family. The Brighton's price was right, and the MOC built a 50-foot-high observation tower on their side of the hill. The Kelly family was so incensed that they began to construct the Gray Tower (known to this day as the spite tower) next door, even as the first tower was under construction, and it blocked the MOC tower view to the west. The MOC then decided to up the ante to 64 feet, warning the Kellys that if they built anything higher, a steel structure of a much greater height would replace MOC's first one. Then the county building inspector stepped into the fray and ruled that for safety reasons neither tower could exceed a height of 64 feet. Today the twin towers still stand, and in 1972 a common top was added to join the two structures, making both of them easily accessible to sightseers.

Above: Climbing the 195.8-foot-high Castle Rock in St. Ignace, Michigan, has been promoted as a tourist attraction since as early as the 1920s.

Below: The Wonder View Tower in Genoa, Colorado; Guin's Longview Tower, along the Mohawk Trail in Greenfield, Massachusetts; and the twin Irish Hills Towers in Onsted, Michigan.

Above: What began as a scenic overlook along the Lincoln Highway in Pennsylvania's Allegheny Mountains evolved into a ship-shaped tourist hotel of great distinction.

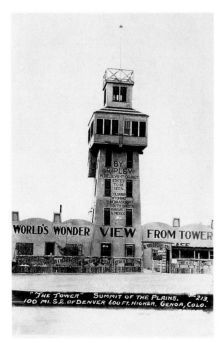

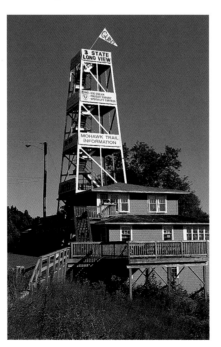

32

100 FT. LONG - 40 FT. HIGH. COLORED LIGHTED. ©by L.A.W. '32'

seats. Thomas Edison and his wife spent their honeymoon here, and William Jennings Bryan was moved to comment, "God could have made something on earth more beautiful, but He did not do so."

The exhilarating experience of viewing the magnificence of nature has prevailed throughout the history of mankind. And so it is not unusual that this experience has been translated into twentieth-century realities that continue to fascinate and inspire people on odysseys of automotive exploration in twentieth-century America.

Left: "The largest Log Entrance of Nature in the World" in Sutherlin, Oregon, is a revelation in and of itself, and one can only imagine the splendor of the hidden view beyond it.

Below: Underwater views are provided in the below-surface theater at the Weeki Wachee Springs Mermaid show in Brooksville, Florida, and at the 450,000 gallon "oceanarium" at Marineland, Florida (bottom), where some 200 portholes provide passing glimpses of creatures of the deep.

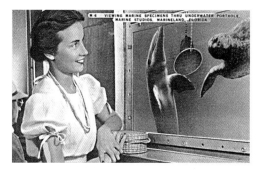

The development of the Grand View Point Lookout in the Allegheny Mountains of Pennsylvania was another complicated affair. It started out as a magnificent panorama on the Lincoln Highway 80 miles east of Pittsburgh at an elevation of 2,464 feet, with a very grand view of three states. In the 1920s a small hotel was hung off this cliff. The hotel was enlarged, and then in 1932 was engulfed in outer walls, which transformed it into an ocean liner in the mountains. It had become the S.S. Grand View Ship Hotel. The ship-shaped building was also a restaurant and souvenir shop. But as it was bypassed by the Pennsylvania Turnpike and then the interstate, the ship became an anachronism, and it now stands in high decay.

In 1946 at Weeki Wachee Springs, Florida, an ex-navy frogman built "the world's only underwater theater and stage" 15 feet below the water's surface. Beginning in 1947, the now-famous live

mermaid show and ballet was premiered with finned bathing beauties (who disappear from view to get some air from hoses strung under the water) performing before audiences of 150 people viewing the productions through thick glass windows looking into the spring.

The same people who now operate Weeki Wachee Springs also run Silver Springs in central Florida. But at Silver Springs there is nary a mermaid in sight. The emphasis here, at this classic Florida attraction, is viewing down into the clear waters from glass-bottom boats to see spring formations and a myriad of marine life. The glass-bottom boat was invented here in 1878 by a man named Hullam Jones, who installed a glass viewing box on the flat bottom of a dugout canoe. Through the years the boats were improved and updated with the addition of gasoline and then electric motors and the installation of canopies and cushioned

ONCE UPON A TIME

Where the magic of Fairyland turns everyone into a child . . .

Storyland *Cape Cod*

A must on your vacation program

ON ROUTE 132 AT HYANNIS
(near the Rotary at Route 28)
Open from 10:00 A.M. to 8:00 P.M.

After World War II, just in time for the baby boomers growing up, a new type of roadside attraction began to evolve — the theme park. In the old days, amusement parks were all about thrill rides, the scarier the better. But then came the "theme park," not so much devoted to rides as to the thematic expression of an idea. Probably first were the Santa Claus parks. Then came amusement experiences that brought fairy-tale tableaux and the characters themselves into real-life existence. The other major theme park idea was the Wild West "Front Street," with other parks concentrating upon the broader idea of Main Street itself.

The Santa Claus and fairy-tale places were targeted toward small children, from about the ages of three or four to seven or eight. The Wild West and Main Streets were said to appeal to slightly older kids, up to, say, age twelve. Santa's Workshop in the Adirondack Mountains of New York State, and Santa places in general, tended to retain that theme only. But the storybook places often added Santa and cowboys as they became larger and larger.

The final step in the evolution of these attractions was to come full circle with the addition of the big-time thrill rides of the amusement parks from which they had evolved. These hybrid parks, which still exist today, strive to be the best of both worlds—fun and games for kids from three to ninety-three. Many of them are showplaces of the first order, immaculately clean and well maintained. Others are funkier and bush league. All coexist along tourist-trodden roadside paths, awaiting families on vacation looking for a novel way to pass two or three hours or a day in idle pursuit of fantasy adventures.

LET'S PRETEND

Like spontaneous combustion, theme parks based upon fairy-tale characters seemed to sprout up nearly simultaneously in several places across the United States in about 1954, predating Disneyland by a year or two. In that year, Charles R. Wood, who already owned resorts in the tourist mecca of Lake George, New York, decided to built a Mother Goose Land on five acres south of the lake on the tourist strip, Route 9. Following his own instincts, and not even knowing if anyone would come, he himself designed and built several nursery rhyme buildings. When he opened for business, the people came.

Right: Two little girls pose beside the Crooked House in the 1960s. It was a popular structure at the Enchanted Forest on U.S. 40 in Ellicott City, Maryland.

Opposite: At Flintstone's Bedrock City, in Valle, Arizona, along the road north to the Grand Canyon, the world of Fred and Wilma and company comes to life. A bunch of small buildings depict landmarks in Bedrock City, including the Beauty Salon and Barber Shop (far left), and Stonehead's General Store (left).

A similar story is told by Bob Morrell. He and his wife, Ruth, were stationed in Germany during the Korean War, and there they met an old German woman who made beautiful dolls. The Morrells bought a lot of them, and the doll maker suggested that when they returned to America that they build a village based on the story of her dolls.

Mr. Morrell came home in 1953 and purchased some land in Glen, New Hampshire. Then he and a construction crew built about fifteen small structures: a shoe, a Three Bears House, a Heidi House, a gift shop, and the like, and in 1954, yes the same year, 1954, Story Land was opened to the public.

A toy designer and former film animator and set designer named Arto Monaco, who had helped early on in creating a Santa theme park in New York State, became the Rembrandt of fantastic fantasy theme parks. To Mr. Monaco, the creation of such attractions became a new career. After helping to conceive Never Never Lands for others, Mr. Monaco decided to build his own pleasure dome behind his home and studio in Upper Jay, New York. The Land of Makebelieve, Arto Monaco's mas-

terpiece, opened up in this tiny mountain town in 1954 (a banner year!), and enthralled children rode around in a small train, drove small-scale Model T Fords, ventured into a humorous jungle of creatures dressed to a tee in all of their finery, and reveled at the splendor of an elaborate fairy-tale castle in which a small visitor could take a seat at King Arthur's round table, or sit on a throne, or even stop by the dungeon.

Illustrator and toy maker Arto Monaco made his dreams come true from 1953 to 1979 at the Land of Makebelieve in the Adirondack Mountains of New York State.

38

LAND OF MAKE BELIEVE ONE RIDE NOT REDEEMABLE NATIONAL TICKET CO., SHAMOKIN, PA. 094009

LAND OF MAKE BELIEVE ONE RIDE NOT REDEEMABLE NATIONAL TICKET CO., SHAMOKIN, PA. 094008

LAND OF MAKE BELIEVE ONE RIDE NOT REDEEMABLE NATIONAL TICKET CO., SHAMOKIN, PA. 094007

LAND OF MAKE BELIEVE ONE RIDE NOT REDEEMABLE NATIONAL TICKET CO., SHAMOKIN, PA. 094006

LAND OF MAKE BELIEVE ONE RIDE NOT REDEEMABLE NATIONAL TICKET CO., SHAMOKIN, PA. 094005

LAND OF MAKE BELIEVE ONE RIDE NOT REDEEMABLE NATIONAL TICKET CO., SHAMOKIN, PA. 094004

But Arto Monaco's attraction was especially charming. His major objective was to design a child-friendly environment. Children were encouraged to touch, feel, sit in, wind up, and participate in the park where Monaco hoped that everything would be "cute and nice." There was the usual assortment of kid-scale nursery rhyme buildings, and an old western town called Cactus Flats, with small ponies pulling an undersize stage coach. The rides were fanciful, not frightening. Each

and every aspect of the park was complete to the smallest details, with Monaco constantly adding a little bit here and a little bit there: a well-considered smile on an alligator statue; real old packaging and a small-scale cracker barrel in the general store; flower-shaped furniture, sink, and mailbox in Mary Mary Quite Contrary's house, and a clockmaker's house where the clocks played music after they had been wound up.

Above: Cinderella and coach stand ready for more riders at the Storytown USA section of the Great Escape Fun Park in Lake George, New York.

Opposite, clockwise from top left: The Pied Piper peddled his wares at Storyland beside the Lincoln Highway in Schellsburg, Pennsylvania. An oft-seen kind of shoe, this humble residence is found at the Magic Forest in Lake George, New York. The Hare is seen here losing the race to the Tortoise at the Great Escape Fun Park, Lake George, New York. In one neat leap, Jack jumps over the candlestick at Deer Acres in Pinconning, Michigan.

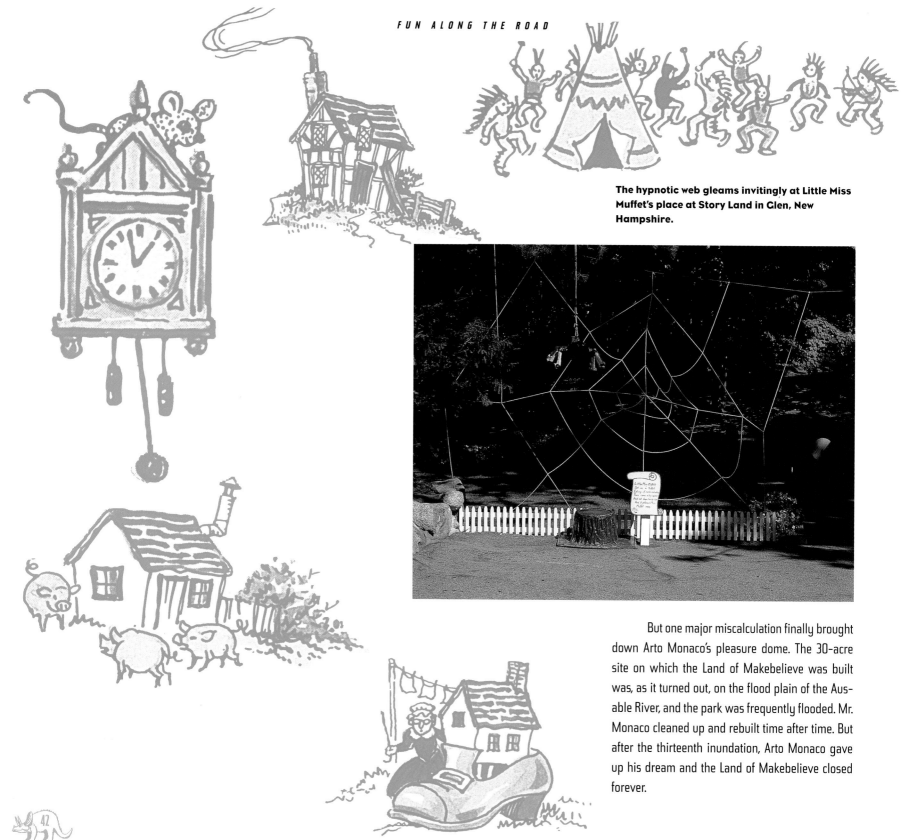

The hypnotic web gleams invitingly at Little Miss Muffet's place at Story Land in Glen, New Hampshire.

But one major miscalculation finally brought down Arto Monaco's pleasure dome. The 30-acre site on which the Land of Makebelieve was built was, as it turned out, on the flood plain of the Ausable River, and the park was frequently flooded. Mr. Monaco cleaned up and rebuilt time after time. But after the thirteenth inundation, Arto Monaco gave up his dream and the Land of Makebelieve closed forever.

Looking back out of another web is a cheerful 1950s view of the magical world of Storytown USA in Lake George, New York.

Now a cheerful and energetic man in his eighties, Mr. Monaco is resigned to his loss. In his backyard still stands the centerpiece of his magical kingdom, the fairy-tale castle now overwhelmed by vegetation, and with one of the small ponies from the stage coach days, now over forty years old, quietly grazing in front of it.

HO! HO! HO!

While the commercialization of Christmas every day of the year is more than enough to turn some people off, the idea has an almost universal appeal to kids. One Santa business dates back to the 1930s, when, as part of a proposed real estate development called Santa Claus Acres, a woman named Ninon Talbot opened a restaurant called the Christmas Tree Inn, north of Kingman, Arizona. The candy cane–striped building was hard to miss. But the inn became more than a restaurant. In order to amuse children, Mrs. Talbot built a wacky miniature Cinderella's Doll House, a kids' play room with a bent stove-pipe-like chimney, and a white picket fence out front. Next to it were the homes of the Three Little Pigs (the straw house eventually blew away), and an amiable pet burro wandered about the premises.

Top: In this contrived publicity photograph, the people at Marine Studios (now Marineland, Florida, south of St. Augustine) celebrate the Christmas holiday.

Right: A replica of Santa's Workshop in the Adirondack Mountains of New York was built in the Rocky Mountains of Colorado in the 1950s, not far from Pike's Peak, including this entrance gate.

Souvenir Christmas theme hats and stockings are just part of the charm of Santa's Workshop on Whiteface Mountain in the Adirondacks at the North Pole, New York. One of the first of the Santa theme parks, dating from 1949, it has set about to make it Christmas Day all summer long. Set designer and illustrator Arto Monaco undertook his first amusement park designs with developer Julian Reiss at Santa's Workshop, including this opaque watercolor sketch (top right), of Santa's Clock Tower, 1947. A fine team of reindeer (right) are part of a visitor posing area at Santa's Workshop.

But the Christmas Tree Inn wasn't really a "theme park" type of operation. Santa Claus Land in Santa Claus, Indiana (the town itself received its name in 1852, or so the story goes), built by Evansville industrialist Louis J. Koch, was probably the first Santa theme park. It opened in 1946 with a toy shop, toy displays, thematic children's rides, a restaurant, and Santa himself constantly on the premises and available to consult with young visitors.

Santa's Workshop in Wilmington, New York, was opened in the Adirondack Mountains in 1949 by Julian Reiss, a German-American entrepreneur. Reiss was driving with his young daughter, Patty, at Christmastime in 1947, and she told him that she wished that Christmas could take place every day of the year. The idea intrigued Mr. Reiss, who then went into partnership with a man who owned some land on Whiteface Mountain. He called upon Arto Monaco to create a village of quaint and sweet chalet-like buildings scaled down to kid size, so that little visitors could experience adult-like scale. An inner-refrigerated North Pole glistened in the sun. After it opened in 1949, there were traffic jams in the mountains as people flocked from miles around to see Santa in the Adirondacks. The site, in the town of Wilmington, officially changed its name to North Pole, New York, so that letters and parcels sent from there bear that magical postmark.

What began in 1947 as the Santa Claus Juice Bar became a group of buildings called Santa Claus Lane on Highway 101 in Carpinteria, California. There was a miniature train and lots of sweet stuff, including a world-class date milk shake. Santa Claus Lane is still there, but, alas, it has been "fixed up."

Greetings from SANTA CLAUS, ARIZONA

CHRISTMAS TREE INN

★ ★

OLIVES — CELERY — ICEBERG

★

ESKIMO FRUIT COCKTAIL
or
NORTH SEA SHRIMP COCKTAIL

★

POINSETTIA TOMATO SOUP
or
REINDEER and CHICKEN SOUP

★

CHOICE of
CHICKEN A LA SNOW WHITE
MARY'S LITTLE LAMB CHOPS
FILET MIGNON A LA SANTA CLAUS

SNOW SHERBET

★

EVERGREEN SALAD
or
NORTH POLE SALAD

★

CHOICE of
MORNING GLORY ICE CREAM
KRISKRINGLE RUM PIE
FAIRYLAND PIE
STARDUST CAKE

★

DWARF COFFEE
NUTS — MINTS

OB-H2427

Above: The bill of fare at the Christmas Tree Inn in northern Arizona, not far from Boulder Dam, was a magical feast of thematically festive cuisine. The owner of the inn also added some small-scale fairy-tale structures to amuse young visitors in the late 1930s.

Right: Ronald Reagan visited Santa Claus Land in Santa Claus, Indiana, in 1955. He is posing with Louis J. Koch, who opened the attraction in 1946, and Santa.

47

Santa Claus attractions sprang up in post-war America in places as geographically diverse as Alaska, California, Florida, North Carolina, and New Hampshire, and a prototypical roadside business targeted toward children became a mainstay in American commercial culture. Nearly all of them contain the same basic elements: a real live Santa Claus holding forth in his own house, often with Mrs. Claus nearby; real live reindeer or reindeer statues; tunic-clad elves; candy kitchens; a post office; toy stores; gingerbread houses; and other saccharine accouterments.

Two views of Santa's allure along the road: Igloos and candy canes are a broad hint of the fun to be enjoyed at Santa's Village in Jefferson, New Hampshire (right), and Santa greets cars lined up to come to Santa Claus Land in Santa Claus, Indiana (below), in about 1962.

While all of these may seem like too much fudge to sophisticated adults, it's the children who really count. And little kids, who drag along their usually willing parents, are the final arbiters. A personal visit to any Santa's place anywhere is convincing proof that the people who built these places have struck a common chord with the majority of American families in search of Christmas cheer year round.

Left: The Santa Claus House at the North Pole in Alaska started as a trading post in Fairbanks in 1949. In a strange tale about how this place was founded, it seems that the owner of the trading post, Con Miller, found a Santa suit in the store. After the trading post failed, Mr. Miller decided to use that suit to become Kris Kringle himself— in residence year-round at his own house for tourists to visit.

Below: The Magic Forest in Lake George, New York, started out in the 1960s as "Christmas City featuring Santa's Village." It has become a more generic theme park, and one of its Santa statues seems to have an almost maniacal glint it its eyes.

GHOST TOWNS

Nearly every little boy has pretended to be a cowboy, and there are also lots of cowgirls out there. Western life as portrayed on television and in the movies has had a tremendous impact upon the American dream. The people who built and operated roadside attractions realized this as well. As theme parks proliferated, the myths and romantic legends of the Old West were manifested on stage-set Main Streets—the kind of places where the Lone Ranger and Tonto would ride out of town at full gallop after putting the bad guys in their place, usually in their graves or in jail.

The granddaddy of all Wild West Main Streets evolved from a roadside berry stand in Buena Park, California, in 1920. Walter and Cordelia Knott's stand began serving chicken dinners in the 1930s, and in 1940 the Knotts began to build an Old West ghost town as a diversion for restaurant guests waiting in line to tie on a feed bag. Many authentic buildings from old towns in the West were relocated to Knott's Berry Farm, the first one being the Old Trails Hotel from Prescott, Arizona. There is a schoolhouse from Kansas, a jail, and the "Haunted Shack," which first stood in Esmeralda, Nevada. These buildings are located along crooked streets and are filled with antiques.

The Harold Warp Pioneer Village in Minden, Nebraska, is an entirely different type of attraction, but like Knott's Berry Farm, it has imported and reconstructed many authentic old buildings. Harold Warp, a Minden native who lived in Chicago, made his fortune by inventing Flex-O-Glas, a polyethylene food wrap sold as Jiffy Wrap and Jiffy Bags. He used his buildings as a way to document "progress" in the United States by attempting to preserve "one item of a kind of all the things people used in settling and building our nation. With 1830 as a starting date, because that marks the start of our mechanization, I wanted to show the evolution of all the marvels we enjoy today."

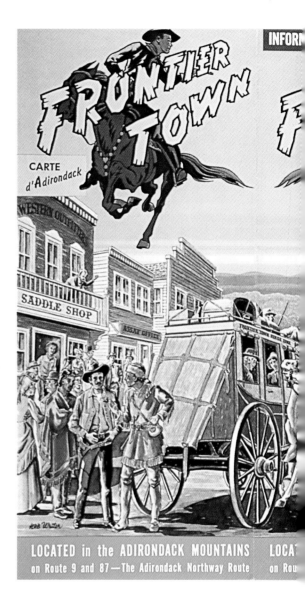

The frontier West first came to New York's Adirondack Mountains in 1955. Frontier Town, in North Hudson, is a place where cliché western movie situations come to life. A bunch of cowboys and cowgirls (left) got caught up in the action as they became part of a stagecoach holdup at Frontier Town in about 1960.

It all begin in 1948 when Mr. Warp, an inveterate collector, first bought the one-room schoolhouse where he had been a student and he then restored it. Then he bought an old Lutheran church, and an old fort. Needing a place to put these, Warp purchased some land on Highway 6 and arranged them and other old buildings around a village green. The village opened in 1953, and soon 500 billboards proclaimed "Nebraska's #1 Tourist Attraction." But Harold Warp collected more than just buildings; he collected nearly everything including kitchen sinks.

Brackettville, Texas native, Happy Shahan, persuaded John Wayne and company to film the movie epic *The Alamo* at his ranch in the late 1950s. An Alamo replica and an entire western village were built (seen in part at top), and they are now promoted as a tourist attraction as well as a film location.

Harold Warp, who made a fortune by inventing and marketing a plastic food wrap in Chicago, never forgot his upbringing and his hometown of Minden, Nebraska. Mr. Warp began to collect artifacts and display them at his Pioneer Village in Minden in the early 1950s. Warp's collection grew to over 50,000 artifacts, and is intended to trace the "history of progress." It is now housed in twenty-six buildings, some of them transplanted and authentically restored.

Now there are huge new exhibition buildings, old buildings, and reproduction buildings, twenty-six of them on twenty acres amidst the cornfields of Nebraska, stocked with over 50,000 artifacts arranged chronologically by type: a transportation exhibit that includes 350 automobiles packed wheel-to-wheel in three large exhibit halls, kitchen appliances, a Hall of Hobbies, Buffalo Bill's saddle, and on and on. Upon his death at age ninety in 1994, Harold Warp had made his collecting hobby a life's work in an endless search to define the history of man's progress.

Another one of these stage-set frontier towns is an actual film location. In Brackettville, Texas, a brash and outgoing rancher named Happy Shahan, then mayor of Brackettville, went out to Hollywood to persuade film studios to make movies in and around his hometown. As he was courting Republic Studios in 1955, Happy Shahan met John Wayne and heard that he was planning to make an epic western about the Alamo. Mr. Wayne, who had been planning to make the movie in Mexico, was wooed to Brackettville by Mr. Shahan. Construction of the *Alamo* sets began on Shahan's thirty-square-mile ranch in 1957, and it was completed two years later. The cost was over one and one-half million dollars for buildings on 400 acres. In addition to a spittin' image of the Alamo itself, an entire western village was erected on land nearby—a complete town with jails, saloons, church, bank, and a blacksmith shop.

Gaslight Village in Lake George, New York, was a somewhat amorphous theme attraction. Its goal was to be entertaining and educational about American culture from about 1875 to 1925. It is seen here in a 1964 watercolor by Robert Vorreyer (above) and a circa 1960 view by photographer Richard K. Dean (right).

After the filming of Wayne's movie was completed, the massive sets have been used as the location for more than sixty motion pictures, television series, and commercials. But the Alamo Village also became a tourist attraction. Happy Shahan placed billboards out on the highways, and when the village is not being used as a location, tourists flock to see this artificial shrine to the Old West.

The Ghost Town at Knott's Berry Farm and the Alamo Village are the most elaborate expressions of Old West culture marketed to the tourist trade, unusual because they are so large and complex. Most frontier lands are a single line of small-scale buildings, and they are full of gift shops, board sidewalks, "Boot Hill" cemeteries, dust, western theme statues, and authentic and reproduction artifacts. Many also hire "cowboys," sometimes on horseback, sometimes not, to stage showdowns and shoot-outs, and to engage in cap pistol duels with young buckaroos.

Clockwise from top left: Three lonely little stage-set buildings on the prairie are a part of the Fort Markley Trading Post along Highway 36 in Seneca, Kansas. Many of the Old West goings-on at this remote location, "West of the Pecos," are promoted, including the Hangman's Tree at Judge Bean's Court in the town of Langtry, Texas. A real-life "shoot-out" is just waiting to be reenacted along the Old West Main Street of Six Gun City in Jefferson, New Hampshire.

SMALLER THAN LIFE

While the ghost town type of attractions brought an Old West Main Street back to life, there were impresarios and artists at work with an even broader purview. Their task, as they defined it, was to create entire villages at a small scale, and then display them, inside or outside, to throngs of tourists. For the many of us who owned and operated our own electric train sets when we were children, this idea has an understandable appeal. For the people who created entire miniature metropolises, children at heart, such a little layout in a recreation room or a basement was just the first step in a much larger endeavor.

Laurence T. Gieringer was one of these men compelled by miniature replicas, and his vision and dedication to his art was vast. At the turn of the century, young Gieringer was fascinated by a hotel perched on a mountaintop, which he could see in the distance in a view from his bedroom window in central Pennsylvania. The five-year-old child set out one day to see for himself what he perceived to be a "toy" building, and in the process, he got lost and spent a frightening night in the woods before being rescued. But this experience didn't dampen his spirit or his growing interest in "toy" buildings. Beginning slowly in 1903, he spent most of his final sixty years turning his boyhood hobby into his life's work by crafting hundreds of little buildings of all types from many eras of American history, and

Laurence T. Gieringer spent much of the last sixty years of his life building "Roadside America," which must be the biggest little city in the USA— an 8,000-square-foot village displayed in a large building in Shartlesville, Pennsylvania.

exhibiting them in a tourist attraction called Road-side America. Located in Pennsylvania Dutch country in Shartlesville, Pennsylvania, between Harrisburg and Allentown, parts of it began to be displayed to local people in 1935, and the entirety of it was moved to a building beside the road and opened as a tourist attraction in 1941. This "largest indoor miniature village" nearly defies description. None of its tourist literature can do it justice; Roadside America has to be seen to be believed. It is an 8,000-square-foot tour de force of more than 300 miniature structures within a fully landscaped set-ting. There are buildings spanning the history of American architecture, along with streetscapes, rivers and streams, toy trains, sound and special lighting effects, 10,000 hand-made trees (many made by Mrs. Gieringer), and 4,000 little people engaged in their everyday pursuits. Laurence Gieringer died in 1963, with his never-to-be-com-pleted little village remaining today as it was upon his death.

The Miniature City, One of the Features of Clinch Park. Traverse City, Michigan

Top: George Turner (second from left) began Tiny Town in Morrison, Colorado, by building a play-house for his daughter in 1915. By 1927, when Mr. Turner sold the property, there were 125 buildings in Turner's Tiny Town and a miniature train, with nearly a mile of track interconnecting them. A loving restoration can now be viewed at the site.

Left: The Miniature City at Clinch Park in Traverse City, Michigan, was a 1932 scale model of the city itself built as a WPA project. Sadly, it deteriorated over its forty-year lifetime. But the original model has been re-created and it will now be displayed indoors.

MIDGET CITY, U.S. 17 & 92 BETWEEN SANFORD & ORLANDO, FLA. 1705

George Turner, a moving company owner, began what was to become Tiny Town in 1915 when he built a playhouse for his daughter near their home on Turkey Creek near the town of Morrison, Colorado, twenty-one miles from Denver. His next building was a replica of his moving company warehouse in Denver. Local people flocked to see these little buildings, and the site was opened to the public in 1920. Before long there were 125 buildings in Turner's Tiny Town, a church, storefronts, a gas station, mining buildings, and many residences. Mr. Turner wired the town for electricity and con-

structed a nearly mile-long miniature railway, which wended its way among the buildings.

After Mr. Turner sold the property in 1927, the attraction fell on hard times. It changed ownership five times, there were three floods, a fire, and the highway passing by it was rerouted in 1948. By the 1980s this once proud tiny village was abandoned and in ruins, and only about one-third of the original buildings were still standing.

But then a broad-based community effort was launched to save and restore Mr. Turner's passion to its former glory. A nonprofit organization was

formed, and little real estate plots were auctioned off to various bidders, who then restored, reconstructed, or built new replicas, mostly in one-sixth scale, of over 100 buildings within urban, rural plains, and hillside settings. Once again it is a joyful destination for children and their parents, open to the public from May to October, and daily from Memorial Day to Labor Day. Mr. Turner would be proud to know that his dream has once again won the hearts of new generations of tourists quite content to admire and relish some of the smaller pleasures in life.

Littleville A miniature town, Chesterton, Ind.

Opposite: Only fragmentary information could be learned about the Midget City in Casselberry, Florida. The builder, seen here, spent six years, probably just after World War II, working on the wooden models. It was sold and moved up the road in 1954, and then sold again four years later and removed from public view.

Above and right: Littleville, a miniature town in Chesterton, Indiana, began as a single building in William Murray's backyard in 1932. Littleville kept getting bigger, and it was moved as it grew to 80 buildings by 1937, and 125 by 1939, set within a grid of narrow concrete streets (above). Eventually, Mr. Murray moved away and Littleville disappeared by the 1960s. But one authentic little building is still preserved in a local backyard.

CHAPTER 4

Opposite: James Sterling, who trapped and raised animals for their fur in Alaska, came east and set up two fur farms, one in Ausauble, New York, in 1920, and a second a year later in Lake Placid, seen here in the 1950s. Fur farms evolved into roadside attractions because many people were interested in seeing the animals themselves. The Sterling-Alaska Fur and Game Farm became known as the "Home of 1000 Animals" when many other species were added to the attraction.

ZOO PARADE

The coinhabitants of our planet—birds, beasts, and marine life, of every size, shape, and description—have always dazzled us. Wild animals were depicted on murals on the walls of caves, and zoos and menageries are a part of the history of civilization. Companion animals, dogs and cats, have been kept and treasured through the eons as well. It is therefore not surprising that many of the most popular roadside amusements were devoted to the animal kingdom.

Probably the most common of the animal attractions were zoos displaying a wide variety of species. Petting zoos were often a logical added attraction at storybook places: little children could see and touch Mary's Little Lamb or the cow, before or after it had jumped over the moon.

There are "game farms" as well. The Sterling-Alaska Fur and Game Farms, with two locations in the Adirondack Mountains of New York State, billed themselves as "homes of 1000 animals." They were not only zoos of many species, but also breeding grounds for animals used to make fur coats and exotic rugs. There were numerous specialty animal places, as well: a Prairie Dog Town near Oakley, Kansas; Tommy Bartlett's Deer Ranch at Silver Springs, Florida; a Buffalo Ranch on Route 66 in Afton, Oklahoma; and the Catalina Island Bird Park off the coast of California.

Bootsie Hurd and her Pets, California Wild Animal Farm, Los Angeles, California.

Top: Animals have continued to have an endless and universal fascination, and they have been the basis of tourist attractions from very early on. Bootsie Hurd shows off some not very wild-looking ponies at the California Wild Animal Farm in Los Angeles, California, circa 1915 to 1920.

Right: Places that trained and kept various species of beasts for use in making movies would sometimes run an attraction out of their home base—in this case the World Jungle Compound, "Home of the Motion Picture Animal Actors," in Thousand Oaks, California.

Creatureland

Left top: A nimble buffalo struts its stuff at the Buffalo Ranch on Route 66 in Afton, Oklahoma.

Left bottom: Little Johnnie Shadoin takes a slow and steady ride aboard a 650-pound giant Galapagos tortoise at Creatureland in Pompano Beach, Florida.

Below: On the way to the beach in Wilmington, North Carolina, a lion beckons to all who might dare enter the Tote Em In Zoo.

IT'S FOR THE BIRDS

Ostrich farms were a curious tourist attraction in the early twentieth century, and the most famous of them were found in Southern California. Edwin Cawston started his operation in South Pasadena in 1886 when he imported a flock of fifty birds from Africa. The major purpose of Cawston's Ostrich Farm was to raise the birds and sell products using "only the finest feathers from the male birds." Cawston's merchandise included plumes, fans and boas, stick-ups and fancies, bands for flounces and gown trimming, hats, novelties, and "adornments beyond number and of every description."

Because these big birds were such exotic creatures, ostrich farms were also promoted as places for tourists to visit. Watching the huge feathers being plucked was touted as an especially exciting event, an "entirely painless" operation that occurred after a hood had been placed over a bird's head. Their eating habits, it says in a 1903 brochure, are extremely peculiar: "They will swallow almost anything—gimlets, lighted pipes, tennis balls, nails, bits of glass, pieces of jewelry, and anything else they can swallow is considered part of their legitimate diet."

Top: This entrance to the Cawston Ostrich Farm in South Pasadena, California, circa 1910, presented a serene and elegant image to the public.

Right: Two flapper-era women catch a lift at Cawston's.

A Portion of Salesroom, Los Angeles Ostrich Farm, Lpppos

Los Angeles Ostrich Farm

Above: The primary role of the ostrich farm was the raising, crafting, and selling of products made from ostrich feathers. The salesroom at the Los Angeles (California) Ostrich Farm was very swank. The grounds of the farm were full of people there to see the ostriches themselves as well as to purchase feathery finery.

Right: Feeding time was a popular time at the Los Angeles Ostrich Farm. In a 1931 letter to her young son describing her visit to an ostrich farm in Los Angeles, California, one woman reported, "The ostriches swallow oranges whole and you can see the ball rolling down their neck."

While ostriches were promoted because they were so large and so strange, other types of birds became popular for other reasons. It would be hard to argue that any living creatures on earth are more colorful and magnificent than tropical birds with their finery of brilliantly colored plumage and their distinctive and often unusual profiles.

Parrot Jungle and Gardens, located within twenty acres of lush jungle foliage in Miami, Florida, is the perfect place to view nearly 1,000 tropical birds and over 1,200 varieties of exotic plants. It was opened in 1936 by Austrian-born Francis S. Scherr, who cut winding paths through the foliage and bought his first shipment of twenty-five birds from a supplier in Laredo, Texas. For an ad-

mission charge of twenty-five cents, Scherr himself would show visitors through his tropical paradise.

By the early 1940s his gardens included Flamingo Lake, where a flock of more than fifty Caribbean pink flamingos could be found, often standing gracefully upon one leg with their heads tucked under a wing. A recent Flamingo Lake flock could be seen in the opening sequence of the popular television series *Miami Vice*. A world-class performing-bird show was added to the festivities in the 1950s. But there are more than just birds at this classic Florida attraction: reptiles (giant tortoises, snakes, turtles, and alligators), mammals such as raccoons, opossums, deer, and skunks, and other exotic creatures such as orangutans, chimpanzees, and gibbons share the jungle with their fine feathered friends.

Opposite: This bird's-eye view drawing from a 1950-vintage brochure for Parrot Jungle and Gardens in Miami begins to capture some of the special charm and elegance of this Florida tourist attraction. Paths run in and around lush tropical foliage, where many species of birds and other animals are on display.

Above: The cover of the same brochure shows the old, masonry entrance building no longer used, but still standing at roadside down from the new entranceway.

Left: Sir Winston Churchill visited Parrot Jungle not once but twice in two days in about 1950. He is seen here with Butch, the sulphur-crested cockatoo, and other friends.

KING OF THE BEASTS

Another popular and unusual animal attraction in Southern California in the 1920s and 1930s was Gay's Lion Farm in El Monte, thirteen miles east of Los Angeles. Here, on five acres, were found over 200 African lions, with 100,000 square feet of arenas and nine lion houses. Charles Gay, whose farm is described in his own brochure as "his pleasure, joy, and happiness," actually had other, contradic-tory, feelings about his feline charges. In an article he wrote for *Modern Mechanix and Inventions* magazine in 1933, Mr. Gay expresses less than mixed emotions about these wild cats: "The most brilliant lion, I have learned during a decade spent in this queer business, displays less intelligence than the commonest dog. . . . Behind their usually calm eyes lurks great, and sometimes immediate danger. . . . While I make no effort to train these brutes, I do have frequent occasion to mingle with as many as 20 in a single group. Early in my career I learned that no lion can be trusted and, also, that their memory is very short indeed. . . . Lions may not be smart, but they are treacherous." Although Mr. Gay feared his lions, he staged shows for the enjoyment of his visitors. In a 1929 postcard mes-

Left: A none-too-treacherous-looking "Numa" poses with Mrs. Gay.

Below left: Mr. and Mrs. Gay were not the only persons working with the lions. Here we see Harry Stewart with "Aladdin" performing a trick.

Below right: Gay's Lion Farm not only supplied animals for use in movies, but also promoted itself with a series of tourist brochures, this brochure cover dating from circa 1930.

sage to her young son, a mother from New Jersey, who was obviously having a fine time, described the goings-on: "We saw Mr. Gay ride a lion and he went into big cages with ten or fifteen lions walking around him. The little ones played hide and seek with him behind logs and were awfully cute."

Opposite: Charles Gay, seen here performing in the ring, had mixed feelings about the lions at this popular Los Angeles-area attraction in El Monte, California, in the 1920s and 1930s. On the one hand he refers fondly to the farm as "his pleasure, joy, and happiness," but Mr. Gay also said of his charges: "Lions may not be smart, but they are treacherous."

GAY'S LION FARM

EL MONTE
CALIFORNIA
NEAR LOS ANGELES

THE BEAR FACTS

CLARK'S ESKIMO SLED DOG RANCH

The Clark family introduced a trained bear show in 1949 at their New Hampshire Trading Post, which continues to be a popular attraction in this White Mountain resort area. Murray Clark is a second-generation member of this family business, and he is seen here as a teenager in the early 1940s (above) with a bear cub, and in his late sixties (opposite, top left) with "Onyx" in 1995.

Bears were among the first animal curiosities to be displayed within view of the motoring public. A magical place with bears, called Clark's Trading Post, began in 1928 as a dog attraction. After Ed Clark had visited Labrador, Newfoundland, in the 1920s and returned to North Woodstock in New Hampshire's White Mountains with a group of purebred Eskimo sled dogs, he and his wife, Florence, opened Ed Clark's Eskimo Sled Dog Ranch. Then they purchased a North American black bear, one of a group of animals that were displayed at the Indian Head, a rock profile just north of them in the Franconia Notch.

More bears were added at the Clarks' attraction in 1935 when a hunter brought them three cubs. They built three pens to display the animals in the late 1930s, and one bear cub named "Ebony" used to pay frequent unscheduled visits to the gift shop in search of sweet goodies in the 1940s. In

1949, Edward and Murray Clark, second-generation members of the Clark clan, began to teach and train the bears, and wondrous bear shows have entertained visitors ever since.

Today, at the bear show at Clark's Trading Post, Murray Clark, now in his late sixties, educates his audiences with the bear facts, and amuses them with an almost nonstop, bearly bearable barrage of bear puns, enough to send nearly anyone to their medicine cabinet for some bear aspirin. Three black bears come bounding into a ring one at a time and perform such amazing feats as walking on top of a barrel, playing basketball, and pushing Murray along in an adult stroller; their efforts are met with rewards of ice cream cones and the "oohs" and "ahs" of delighted spectators. Today, members of the third and fourth generations of the Clark family help to carry on the tradition of this family-owned business.

Left: Spikehorn Meyer, the man with a white beard and flowing white hair seen to the right of his sign, began his career in roadside marketing by opening a field to rent to campers in 1929 in Harrison, Michigan. Spikehorn, a.k.a. "Grizzly Ike," started off his campground with an elk and a buffalo for people to gawk at, but they weren't "friendly" enough. So Spikehorn got some bears as replacements, and his Bear Den thrived into the 1950s.

MONKEY BUSINESS

Human beings have always felt a special fascination about their closest relatives in the animal kingdom—monkeys and their kin. They have become the basis for several popular attractions, and they have also been used as sideshow come-ons for other types of roadside businesses, not unlike the bears beside the tourist highways.

The oldest monkey business in Florida is probably the Monkey Jungle, founded in 1933 by Joseph and Grace DuMond. The DuMonds purchased ten acres of hardwood hummock land in Goulds, twenty-two miles south of Miami—a nearly perfect replica of the monkey's habitat in Southeast Asia.

Mr. DuMond conducted scientific primate research and then began charging ten cents admission in 1935 to assist him in his work. At first there were no barriers erected. But, because some of the primates were territorial, cages were introduced, not to cage the monkeys, but to protect visitors. Today, there are some 300 primates on thirty acres in the place where "the humans are caged and the monkeys run free," although an electric fence surrounds the entire attraction.

Above and above right: Some thirty-three species of primates run free on thirty acres at the Monkey Jungle, twenty-two miles south of Miami, Florida. The DuMond family, which began the attraction in 1933, now has visitors to the Monkey Jungle wandering around in caged corridors to protect both the visitors themselves as well as the inhabitants.

Right: At the Frontier Fort in Wilmington, North Carolina, in 1985, a "Feed the Monkeys" cage was only one of the major roadside lures intended to bring motorists to a halt.

D-261—Monkey at Monkey Jungle, South of Miami, Florida

MONKEY BUSINESS

an
INFORMATIVE
SOUVENIR

MONKEY ISLAND

3300 CAHUENGA BLVD. "ON THE PASS"
HOLLYWOOD, CALIFORNIA

Profusely Illustrated ◆ 15c.

The most elaborate monkey operation in the West was a place called Monkey Island located along the Cahuenga Pass in Hollywood, California, in the 1930s and 1940s. The attraction featured barrels and barrels of monkeys, over 500 of them, including "Coy," the chimpanzee from the Johnny Weissmuller *Tarzan* movies. All of the primates lived on an oval-shaped island surrounded by a fifteen-foot-wide, water-filled moat.

Above: A souvenir booklet cover for Monkey Island in Hollywood, California, suggests the "volcano island" on which 500 primates lived and where tourists were encouraged to feed the primates by tossing food to them across a water moat.

Left: A chimp in a go-kart was but one of the extra added attractions at the Sterling-Alaska Fur and Game Farm in Lake Placid, New York.

71

FLIPPER'S FRIENDS

Marineland, a landmark Florida attraction located eighteen miles south of St. Augustine, is nearly as well known for its breathtaking "nautical moderne" architecture and landscape architecture as it is for displaying marine life. It was founded by a group of like-minded people, some of whom had ties with some of America's wealthiest families, including W. Douglas Burden, a trustee of the American Museum of Natural History and a great-great-grandson of Cornelius Vanderbilt, his cousin Cornelius Vanderbilt Whitney, also a museum trustee, and Count Ilya Tolstoy, grandson of Leo Tolstoy.

The founding group was interested in building a facility to be used for filming underwater action. They commissioned an architect, M. F. Has-

Below and right: Marine Studios began in 1938 as a place to film finny creatures. It's there to this day as Marineland and is on the National Register of Historic Places, with vestiges of its original 1930s "nautical moderne" design to be seen. The dolphin stadium was built in 1954, and its flying parabolic arches provide a "dome" for the pool used in the performing dolphins show.

DOLPHIN STADIUM

77

brouck, and a landscape architect, Mulford B. Foster, who together designed a complex that contained two "oceanariums," a word they coined to describe these enormous aquariums. The rectangular one displays a variety of saltwater marine species, and the circular tank, 75 feet in diameter and twelve feet deep, is used to stage dolphin feeding exhibitions.

Left: Spectators marvel and sometimes get soaked during the dolphin feeding exhibition at Marineland.

Bottom left: Marineland is distinguished for its landscape architecture as well: a huge shark's jaw is but part of the extraordinary landscape in Whitney Park.

Below: A Marine Studios postcard depicts the humdrum side of life beneath the water. There is also a spectacular display of saltwater fish and other creatures of the deep.

World's only underwater "vacuum cleaner" Marine Studios

Marine Studios, as it was then known, opened to a throng of 20,000 visitors on June 23, 1938. A shallow oblong stadium for performing dolphin shows was added in 1954; sweeping parabolic arches were constructed above it in 1955. Then time stood still at the original site and it has remained nearly unchanged. For many years, this enchanting place also became a gathering place for prominent literary figures, including Ernest Hemingway, John Dos Passos, and Thornton Wilder. Not surprisingly, it has been listed on the National Register of Historic Places.

Left: The giant fiberglass muskie statue (four and one-half stories high) at the National Freshwater Fishing Hall of Fame in Hayward, Wisconsin, was completed in 1979. There are several smaller game fish statues on display as well as various kinds of fishing memorabilia in this serious "hall of fame."

Above: The Blue Whale, located right beside an ark-shaped building, was a great place for a picnic and swim along Route 66 in Catoosa, Oklahoma.

Right: "Happy the Walking Fish," who "walks on land before your very eyes," was part of an attraction south of Daytona Beach, Florida. A brochure handout tells us about the tunnel, the birds, the monkeys, and so on, and then, just to make things perfectly clear, identifies itself as the "Tunnel of Fantasy," also noting that it was formerly known as the "Atomic Tunnel."

REPTILES GALORE

While it's quite easy to understand people's affection for little replicas of human beings cavorting about, or spectacularly hued tropical birds, it's a totally different kind of wonder that enthralls spectators as they observe slithering snakes and prehistoric-looking alligators and crocodiles. It's a sublime difference, like going to the sideshow instead of the circus or going to a horror movie instead of *Mary Poppins*. To satisfy travelers' curiosity and to educate them about these creepy crawlies, snake farms and alligator places have been a mainstay beside the highway since very early on.

Below: August Mack was a talented sculptor. In addition to the Brazen Serpent, which he installed in his own home in Bedford, Indiana, he also created the first Santa Claus statue at the Indiana Santa Claus Land.

Above: Snakeville was a typical highway snake farm located on the once major Highway 99 in Southern California.

Bottom right: Motl's Exhibit of West Texas Rattle Snakes was a roadside attraction on wheels.

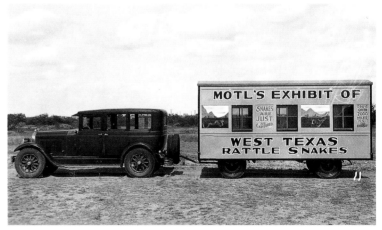

Left: Earl Brockelsby, who founded the Black Hills Reptile Gardens in Rapid City, South Dakota, in 1937, is seen here in 1950 posing with his besnaked nephew, Gaynor Wild.

Below: Along with the glass-bottom boats and the other attractions of Silver Springs, Florida, there was also Ross Allen's Reptile Institute for the none-too-faint-at-heart.

Snake farms, usually set within permanent buildings, but sometimes moving around from place to place in trailers, can be found throughout the United States. Perhaps the definitive example is the Black Hills Reptile Gardens located along Highway 16 between Rapid City and Mount Rushmore in South Dakota. The attraction's founder, Earl Brockelsby, when he worked as a guide at "The Hidden City" in 1935, would remove his hat at the end of the tour to reveal a coiled-up rattlesnake on his head. The next year, to attract tourists to a rock shop, he would stand out by the road and have his partner pretend to photograph him holding a snake. Brockelsby opened a small version of his attraction in 1937, and it expanded to larger quarters in the 1960s. It is now operated by Brockelsby's son, John, and displays "the largest collection of reptiles in the world"— 700 to 800 snakes, lizards, turtles, and crocodiles.

Right: GOMEK, "the largest crocodilian in the western hemisphere," was the supreme attraction at the St. Augustine (Florida) Alligator Farm, from 1989 until his death from heart failure in March of 1997. After a visit to a taxidermist, GOMEK became a less fearsome display at this National Register Florida attraction.

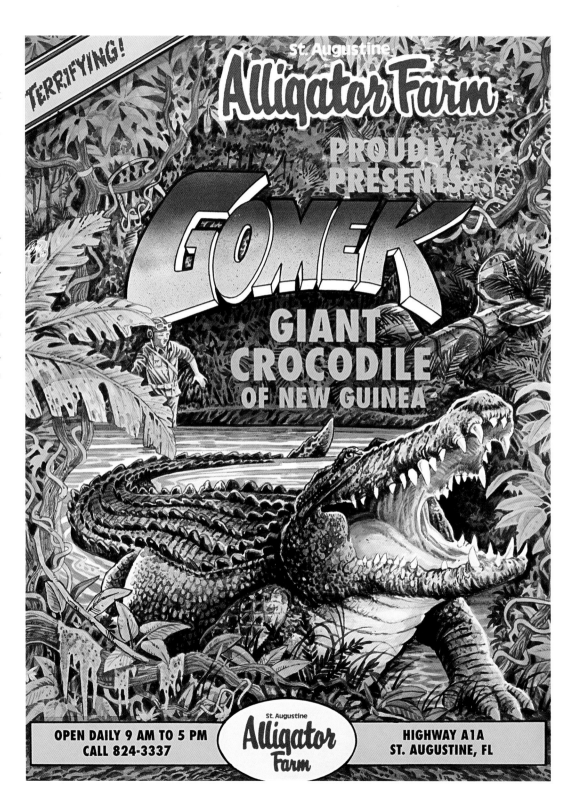

Above: A compelling image was used to promote the not-very-well-known Sea Zoo in Daytona Beach, Florida, in the 1950s.

Right: St. Augustine Alligator Farm Christmas card.

Alligator places have an even longer history. These fascinating, usually sluggish creatures (but watch out when they're in the water and when they're hungry) are most often displayed to tourists in the warm climates that best suit them. The St. Augustine Alligator Farm in Florida is the oldest and most distinguished of these businesses. It was established in 1893 by George Reddington and Felix Fire when they were operating a trolley from the city to its beaches several miles away. Along the way, tourists often encountered alligators, and Reddington and Fire decided to capitalize upon their fascination by capturing some of them and placing them on exhibit in an abandoned beach house. The "farm" was moved to more expansive quarters in 1922, and now visitors can see 1,400 alligators and crocodiles, all twenty-two known living species of them. In 1993 the St. Augustine Alligator Farm was placed on the National Register of Historic Places because of the design of its quarters and because it is "one of the oldest and most significant tourist attractions in Florida."

Below: A tourist's first move is made quite clear at the Gatorland Zoo's toothy entrance in South Orlando, Florida.

Above: A classic publicity photograph shows a gator getting his act cleaned up at an unidentified Florida attraction from the 1950s — probably either Tropical Hobbyland or Musa Isle in Miami, Florida.

Right: This stogie-toting alligator used to rule Route I at Gatorland just north of St. Augustine, Florida.

DINOSAURS

Prehistoric creatures have always captured our collective imaginations, but children especially are taken with these "monsters." Archaeologists have re-created them as bony sculptures to be found in science museums such as the famed Dinosaur Hall at the American Museum of Natural History in New York City. Not-so-accurate, but fanciful, renditions of these species can be found in dinosaur parks across America. Two of the grandest of these attractions date from the 1930s and can still be found, alive and well, in the upper Midwest.

Dinosaur World, dating from the 1960s, in Eureka Springs, Arkansas, is much larger than most dinosaur parks. A visitor needs to drive from one display to another, getting out of the car for a closer view. Early in the tour one gets to see the very fanciful Dinosaur Nursery (opposite), which has since been removed due to vandalism, then a creature with a pointed head (top left), and yet another looking a lot like a woman's handbag (above).

Left: Thunderbeast Park, not far from Crater Lake in Chiloquin, Oregon, was unusual because it chose to focus upon lesser-known, long-gone species, such as this Uintatherium.

BRONTOSAURUS UNDER CONSTRUCTION IN PAULORR DOMKE'S PREHISTORICAL ZOO GARDENS, OSSINEKE, MICH.

One of them is folk art on a grand scale, located on Highway 23 in Ossineke, Michigan. It was built over a forty-year period by a self-trained sculptor named Paul Domke. Mr. Domke, a deeply religious man, built the thirty-odd figures in the park by hand as a way of trying to integrate the theory of evolution with the Book of Genesis.

The concrete statues of critters scattered throughout the wooded site are extraordinary. The most spectacular is an eighty-five-foot walk-through brontosaurus built in the 1940s. Some of the monsters are depicted attacking one another, with blood oozing from their mouths, and many, although correct in form, were painted with absurd colors. There are cave men and cave women as well, some locked in mortal combat with their monstrous compatriots. Domke died at the age of ninety-four in the early 1980s. But his park lives on in all of its funky glory.

Paul Domke spent four decades constructing some thirty statues at his Dinosaur Gardens in Ossineke, Michigan. The artist was trying, in his own way, to resolve the theory of evolution with the Book of Genesis. The largest statue, seen here both under construction in the 1940s (opposite), and complete in the 1980s (above), is a eighty-five-foot-long, walk-in brontosaurus. In addition to beasts, Mr. Domke also added a few short cave women (left) and cave men to his "Prehistorical Zoo."

Another great dinosaur attraction can be found in Rapid City, South Dakota. It is one of America's oddest public works projects, having been funded by FDR's Works Progress Administration. Because of the increased volume of tourists in the Black Hills, spurred in part by the completion of Mount Rushmore, the Rapid City Chamber of Commerce proposed building a large sculpture on a hill overlooking the city. A local paleontologist came up with the idea of a dinosaur theme, and a local sculptor and lawyer named Emmit A. Sullivan was commissioned to design what turned out to be seven statues widely spaced on the magnificent hilltop site. Today, these statues stand proud in what has become a city park, and they are now listed on the National Register of Historic Places.

Below and right: The Dinosaur Park in Rapid City, South Dakota, began as a WPA project in the 1930s. It survives to this day as a free attraction in a public park.

R-348   THREE DINOSAUR

Left: It seems highly unlikely that this extinct creature was bright yellow, but anything cheerful was perfectly okay at the Enchanted Forest and Prehistoric Land in Wisconsin Dells, Wisconsin.

Bottom left: Recognizing how primeval-looking the praying mantis is, the people who built the Prehistoric Forest in Onsted, Michigan, decided to include one along with a variety of other species.

Below: Two huge dinosaurs, built in the 1970s and 1980s, loom large in the desert by the interstate at the Wheel Inn in Cabazon, California, near Palm Springs.

CHAPTER 5

MADE BY HAND

Below and right: Ole S. Quammen, an amateur geologist who worked for the Independent Oil Company, decided to distinguish his hometown of Lemmon, South Dakota, by building the Petrified Wood Park in the early 1930s. He hired crews of workers who hauled tons and tons of petrified materials to the site and built 380 fossilized monuments, including 100 cone-shaped pyramids and round stones called "cannon balls."

PETRIFIED WOOD SIGN NEAR LEMMON, SOUTH DAKOTA.

Among the most fascinating of all roadside attractions are those which have been created by artists. The form and type of these creations are myriad. What they share in common is a dedication of vision and self-expression. Their appeal is similar to the experience of visiting a "real" museum: to see, appreciate, and be inspired by the artist's skill and vision.

Some of these artistic achievements were inspired by religious beliefs, others by even more cosmic ideas. Still others were singular and idiosyncratic works of craftsmanship.

The Petrified Wood Park in Lemmon, South Dakota, dedicated in 1932, is very special for several reasons. It was the vision of a local businessman, Ole S. Quammen, a Norwegian immigrant who wanted to put his adopted home town on the map. Mr. Quammen, an amateur geologist, was aware of the large amount of fossilized remains that existed in the western Dakotas. In 1930, without outside knowledge or capital, he began building his extraordinary artistic

statement. Working under the supervision of Mr. Quammen, thirty to forty local men hauled massive quantities of petrified remnants to the site by wagon. What they built is a veritable believe-it-or-not of sculptural achievement. The park contains 3,700 tons of petrified wood, 250 tons of petrified grass, and 13,000 petrified bones, and all of this was used to create: 100 cone-shaped pyramids, 7 to 32 feet high and up to 15 feet in diameter, interspersed with "cannon balls," round stones ranging in size from one-half inch to several feet in diameter; 380 individual fossilized monuments; and 600 tons of unassembled fossilized material.

GEO. DAYNOR
STONE AGE MUSIC
PALACE DEPRESSION Vineland, N.J.

George Daynor (left), an eccentric artist, came to Vineland, New Jersey, in 1929 to build a house to get himself through the Great Depression. He constructed his Palace Depression from found materials (below), and when it was completed, opened it to the public in 1932. The strange residence was also reproduced on a hand-tinted Christmas card (bottom).

PALACE DEPRESSION VINELAND, N.J.

George Daynor, a drifter with a "dream," is one of several strong-willed and self-trained artists who built themselves a house and then opened it to the public as an attraction. But what a house and what a strange man! It seems that the artist was hitchhiking back from Alaska in 1929 when he had a "vision" instructing him to go to New Jersey and to build himself a safe haven to get him through the depression. He was given permission to settle on a swampy site in Vineland, New Jersey, where an automobile junkyard had once been located. Daynor built his house, which he called the "Palace Depression," using materials he found on the land itself and in junkyards: automo-

bile parts, rocks, logs, and clay. The result, as described in his own promotional literature, was "the greatest idea of originality ever conceived in the history of the world by one man with his two hands."

The Palace Depression was opened free of charge to the public on Christmas Day, 1932. By the 1940s the Palace had begun to deteriorate, and Daynor couldn't keep up with the maintenance and recurring vandalism. Mr. Daynor died in 1964 at the age of eighty-six. The property was purchased by the city, and his palatial dream was torn down to make way for a park.

PALACE DEPRESSION
VINELAND, N. J.

Interior of the Paper House - Made Entirely of newspapers - Pigeon Cove, Mass.
Mr. and Mrs. E. F. Stenman the originator.

Left: In 1922, Elis F. Stenman decided to experiment with old newspapers, and he began to prepare a newspaper building material by gluing layer after layer together and then subjecting the paper to two tons of pressure. The result was the Paper House in Pigeon Cove, Massachusetts—the house itself and all the furnishings were made with "recycled" newsprint.

SIX BEAUTIFUL VIEWS IN FULL COLOR

Greetings from

SAILOR TOM'S

NAUTICAL HOME
Tom
See the House that Jack Built

READING, MASS.

Open for Inspection on Request — Small Admission Charge

MAY YOUR CRUISE THROUGH LIFE BE A PLEASANT ONE — Sailor Tom

SHIP'S GALLEY

Sailor Tom's ship-shaped home in Reading, Massachusetts, was an added attraction for visitors to his nearby restaurant. Patrons and others could pay a fee to visit Tom and Polly Thompson's residence in all of its nautical splendor, and the proprietors even issued an envelope of souvenir postcards to help people to recall their experience.

Edward Leedskalnin, a Latvian native, was said to have built the Coral Castle in Homestead, Florida, as an act of devotion to his fiancée, who had jilted him. He sculpted and carved over 1,100 tons of coral rock, opening his work in progress to the public in 1925. Unlike the religious grottoes, Coral Castle was "cosmic" in its intent. Celestial and mystical imagery abounds, and the siting and the sculptures are aligned with the moon and the sun. In a postcard view (above right), a woman cools off in a coral rock bathtub.

There were many other artists and craftsmen working on a smaller scale who then put the fruits of their labor on display for public viewing, and a man named Raymond W. Overholzer perfectly fits this mold. Mr. Overholzer, a hunting and fishing guide in central Michigan, had a consuming passion for woodcarving. As he wandered through the woods, he became distressed at the leftover pieces of white pine abandoned by lumbermen. And so he began to drag pieces of it—stumps, roots, and branches—back to his home in the small town of Baldwin. Beginning in 1935, Mr. Overholzer began displaying pieces of furniture he had made entirely by hand in his own home. By 1941 he'd created so many pieces of furniture that he built a 2,500-square-foot building, which became the Shrine of the Pines.

Raymond W. Overholzer, appalled by wasted and discarded pieces of white pine lumber, began to drag them home, and he then used this wood to craft pieces of furniture entirely by hand.

RASMUS PETERSEN

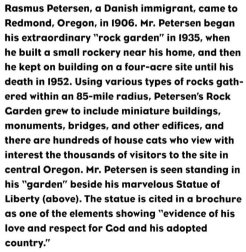

Rasmus Petersen, a Danish immigrant, came to Redmond, Oregon, in 1906. Mr. Petersen began his extraordinary "rock garden" in 1935, when he built a small rockery near his home, and then he kept on building on a four-acre site until his death in 1952. Using various types of rocks gathered within an 85-mile radius, Petersen's Rock Garden grew to include miniature buildings, monuments, bridges, and other edifices, and there are hundreds of house cats who view with interest the thousands of visitors to the site in central Oregon. Mr. Petersen is seen standing in his "garden" beside his marvelous Statue of Liberty (above). The statue is cited in a brochure as one of the elements showing "evidence of his love and respect for God and his adopted country."

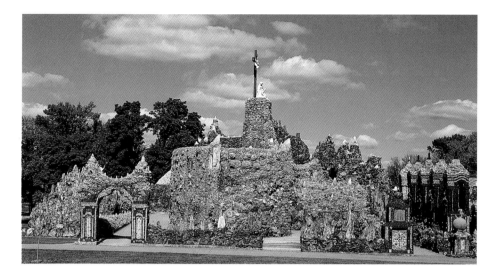

"EUCHARISTIC ALTAR", IN CEMETERY AT DICKEYVILLE, WIS.

THE BUILDER AT WORK
DICKEYVILLE, WIS.   3
(J. SEIDL PHOTO)

Above: Father Paul Dobberstein arrived in West Bend, Iowa, in 1898 and spent the remaining fifty-seven years of his life building the Grotto of Redemption. The grotto highlights man's redemption, from the Garden of Eden to the Twelve Stations of the Cross to the Resurrection itself. As people came to see Father Dobberstein at work, they left donations, and thus this religious statement became a roadside attraction.

Right: The Dickeyville Grotto in Dickeyville, Wisconsin, was also built of stone, mortar, and other natural materials. Father Mathias Wernerus labored from 1925 to 1930 building several shrines, gardens, fences, and other elements (the Eucharistic Altar in the cemetery is seen at top). More than 60,000 visitors a year flock to this tiny Wisconsin town to marvel at the father's work.

Mr. and Mrs. Postage Stamp
Nettie and Alice Museum of Hobbies
Hiway 60-70-99 Beaumont, Calif.

Above: Only fragmentary information and photographic postcards remain as evidence of the Nettie and Alice Museum of Hobbies in Beaumont, California. A Beaumont native remembers Nettie and Alice, two elderly women who made, collected, and displayed dolls and other toys in their "museum" at roadside. In addition to Mr. and Mrs. Postage Stamp, seen here, there was another doll couple on exhibit, identified as "Mr. and Mrs. Rare Button (15,000)."

Right: A visit to E. P. Faustman's Miniature Carnival was a charming way to pass some time in Aurora, Nebraska, in the late 1940s.

E. P. Faustman's Miniauture Carnival

AURORA NEBR.

MEMORIAL CLOCK TO
ANTONIN DVORAK

The Bily Brothers
Spillville, Iowa

THE VILLAGE BLACKSMITH

MUSEUM OF WOODCARVING SPOONER, WIS. 2-A-552

Top: Frank and Joseph Bily, of Spillville, Iowa, loved to spend their leisure time carving wooden clock cases, busts, statuettes, and plaques, with Joseph Bily doing the designing and joining, while his brother did the carvings. The violin clock (left) was created to commemorate Antonín Dvořák's visit to Spillville in 1893. The Bily Brothers Clock Museum is still open to the public from May to October.

Above: The Museum of Woodcarving in Spooner, Wisconsin, "is the largest collection of wood carvings in the world created by one man—Joseph T. Barta." These six small dinosaur carvings in their own tableau are just the tip of the iceberg. Barta's nephew and his wife still operate the museum, which contains 100 life-size figures and more than 400 miniature figures created by Mr. Barta over a thirty-year period.

97

CHAPTER 6

PUTTERING AROUND

Opposite: Miniature golf has become a gigantic activity beside the freeways of California as can be seen at Storybook Land Golf in San Diego, California. The huge castle in the background is a lure to tempt motorists to exit at the next off-ramp.

A short "Course" to a heart

OF "COURSE" I WANT YOU FOR MY VALENTINE

Miniature golf began to evolve in the 1920s, and by now this innocent take-off of the grand and venerable game has tapped into the very ethos of our culture. It's the kind of family experience where a son or daughter can beat Mom or Dad straight up from day one or a "safe date" for teenagers.

Just where and when this popular phenomenon began is difficult to precisely ascertain, although there is published evidence that a man had a small putting course built on his private estate in Pinehurst, North Carolina, by 1916. By the mid to late 1920s, little putting courses with obstacles were cropping up on vacant lots in downtown areas, on the rooftops of city office buildings, and along the road. A major problem with many of these early courses was perfecting the putting surface itself. But a man named Thomas Fairbairn, who owned a cotton gin and who wished to build a small golf course of his own, looked down and noticed the cottonseed hulls that had been crushed down into an even surface beneath workers' feet. He envisioned a workable putting surface and quickly patented his smooth idea—crushed cottonseed hulls bound with oil and then dyed green. This unlikely formulation worked really well for the burgeoning game, and soon "The Madness of 1930" spread across the United States like wildfire. Grantland Rice, in a late 1930 article in *Collier's* magazine titled "Small Game Hunters," marveled at this new pastime: "And then almost before anyone

knew what had happened midget golf courses appeared all over the landscape. . . . They became thicker than blooms in a daisy field, and thousands of addicts are playing day and night—all day and all night in many places."

The formal founding of miniature golf is said to have taken place on Lookout Mountain in Tennessee when Garnet and Frieda Carter were creating their real estate development for the wealthy called Fairyland. Evidently, as one version of the story goes, the assembled new homeowners became impatient for the construction of a real golf course to be completed. The Carters constructed a miniature golf course in 1929 with assorted statues of gnomes and elves scattered about. The golfers and others, including children, couldn't get enough of this little game. Seeing that he was on to a good thing, Garnet Carter patented his idea as a chain of little links called Tom Thumb Golf, and suddenly there were hundreds and hundreds of layouts across the nation.

Silly palm-frond birds were part of the atmosphere at the Wilshire Birdie Links in Los Angeles about 1930.

No. 05 SPORT PILLOW J.B.K Co. F-30

Left: A beautiful miniature golf pillow cover is partial evidence that this tiny game became a fad called "The Madness of 1930."

Below: The Eskimo Village theme course in Los Angeles in 1930 was replete with arctic imagery—including igloos, polar bears, and lots of stucco icicles everywhere.

At the Tom Thumb courses, as well as at thousands of others, the emphasis was on designing eighteen tricky little passages with frustrating obstacles through which the ball had to be skillfully hit in order to get a hole in one or two strokes, or even to get the ball into the hole at all. But there were other types of obstacles, sculptural objects, which gave an even more distinct look to the game. A cliché vocabulary of such obstacles evolved from nearly day one. Models of generic buildings, such as castles, lighthouses, and the classic miniature golf windmill, were scattered about the courses. Sometimes these objects had a functional purpose as an obstruction, as in having to hit a ball through a windmill when a blade wasn't blocking the route. At other times, the function of these objects was purely symbolic and entertaining. But in addition to being objects of amusement or consternation to the putters, these large statues served another vital function as roadside lures to attract potential customers passing by in their cars.

SCENE AT NORTON'S Miniature GOLF COURSE - HOLSTEIN-Ia.

Above left: Little Dorothy Messina plays the fourth hole at the Rinkiedink Miniature Golf Course in Ozone Park, New York. The course was operated on a vacant lot by a twelve-year-old entrepreneur named Julius Hamilton, who built his layout from "found" materials such as drainpipes, old tires, and scrap wood.

Above: The windmill at the miniature golf course at Lucy's Amusement Park in Minot, North Dakota, is a work of folk art handcrafted by its owner, Lucy Cork.

Left: Putters were backed up to play a round at Norton's Miniature Golf Course in rural Holstein, Iowa.

Opposite left: A 1930-era comic postcard shows that the great fad had spread throughout the United States.

Opposite right: In an original watercolor postcard sent by Kevin Kutz in 1994, the artist portrays the charmingly typical links at a KOA Campground in the Delaware Water Gap area of Pennsylvania.

By 1930 there were some 25,000 to 50,000 layouts, nearly everywhere. The initial bubble burst and the craze went into remission, but the game had become ingrained as a silly but pleasant way to while away the hours. Little courses, fewer in number, continued to flourish in the 1930s. Moms and Pops and even children set up shop at curbside—usually crude layouts for a nickel or a dime a round. People stopped and played.

The second renaissance of miniature golf took place after World War II as downtown areas began to give way to suburban developments. Along the highway strips that connected the old main streets to the suburbs, myriad highway businesses and attractions began to spring up, including many new miniature golf courses.

The third wave of miniature golf began in the 1960s. The old-fashioned formula of object hazards within and upon the courses continued, but with an new and outrageous vigor, both in increased scale and an increasingly bizarre content. At places called Goofy Golf, Wacky Golf, and Goony Golf, located primarily in the Southeast, nothing was sacred. Many of the great icons of mankind have been caricatured and pressed into service in these mazes of artificial delight—churches, pagodas, Buddhas, and totem poles.

But the decades beginning with the 1960s were also a period of gigantic developments and innovations. As the interstate highway system bypassed the earlier automotive strips, a new breed of courses began to appear. They were much larger in scale, and the hazards became much more enormous, so that people speeding by at 55 or 65 miles per hour could discern what was going on, and then exit at the next off-ramp. The multimillion courses along the freeways of Southern California, many constructed by Mormon master builders, were often three or four courses spread across vast areas of frontage land beside the superhighways.

Left: The unlikely centerpiece of Espey and Daly's Hi-Land Miniature Golf in St. Louis, Missouri, is the symbol of Bob's Big Boy Hamburgers gone astray.

Below: In miniature golf nothing is sacred. At Wacky Golf in Myrtle Beach, South Carolina, a red-robed Buddha has been conscripted to serve as an obstacle.

The other major explosion of miniature golf madness took place in Myrtle Beach, South Carolina. Although the tiny game had been a popular draw at resort destinations from its very beginnings, what happened in the Myrtle Beach area, along a fifty-mile-long strip called Kings Highway, almost defies a logical explanation. There, located nearly cheek-by-jowl, can be found dozens and dozens of fabulous miniature golf courses, the next one even more amazing than the one previously passed. The game of miniature golf itself had become a major destination activity for tourists at Myrtle Beach.

But something else extraordinary happened at Myrtle Beach—an entirely new design idea was perfected, probably first used in a chain called Jungle Golf. Here is how it worked. A small lake was excavated at roadside, and the dirt dug out to form the lake was used to build a mountain behind the water. The mountain was given further strength and definition by laying down chicken wire and then covering it with sprayed rock. A series of gullies and streams was built around and through the mountain, and a water pumping system was used to create waterfalls and streams on the mountain emptying into the lake, and then the water was recirculated. The miniature golf holes themselves, often without functional hazard symbols, were built on the flat land around the lake and up, in, and through the mountain.

Right: Onion domes galore are part of the ecclesiastical centerpiece at Rainbow Falls Golf in Myrtle Beach, South Carolina.

Bottom right: A freaked-out tree monster is an imposing obstacle at Sir Goony Golf in Chattanooga, Tennessee.

Below: An unfaltering Humpty Dumpty helps to show the way at Tower Tee Mini Golf in St. Louis, Missouri.

Today, miniature golf is a popular if not strenuous recreational alternative at resorts and beside highways across America. Although it is not the national craze that it was during its heyday in the 1930s, a large throng of devotees, putters in hand, can be found waiting to play 18, 36, or even 72 holes of miniature mayhem. Usually the game is played on artificial mountains beside ponds. There are also some adult variations where the game has evolved into a game of true skill, with devilishly difficult layouts with real sand and water hazards. And occasionally, but rarely, one can still find a Mom-and-Pop survivor from the 1950s, with individually crafted, primitive folk-art-like hazards, and soggy carpets, and a snack bar dispensing soft ice cream and hot dogs. But whatever the set-up, one thing is for certain. "The Madness of 1930," which just wouldn't go away, is certain to continue being a popular form of roadside amusement for many years to come.

Left: This difficult-appearing hole at Jungleland Miniature Golf in Atlantic Beach, North Carolina, is less daunting than it appears to be, since all channels lead right to the hole.

Opposite top: Miniature golf becomes a game of intricate skill at Legendary Golf in Ormand Beach, Florida. This hole is reminiscent of the island-type par threes negotiated by the pros as seen in televised golf tournaments.

Left: Hole number 10 at the real turf course called Hutsie Putsie in Deposit, New York, is a long short story. The ball is placed on a tee, and the putter is used as a driver to get across a water hazard. A screen behind the hole prevents the ball from being driven to kingdom come. All of this action takes place in less than ten feet.

Above: The Jungleland Miniature Golf course in Atlantic Beach, North Carolina, is a typical example of the "Myrtle Beach" style of the little game. The landfill excavated to create the lake was used to create a mountainous terrain on which the holes are arranged, and the dyed lake water is pumped up the mountain and recirculated back in a waterfall.

GIFT SHOPS

Probably the most prevalent, and perhaps the most unnecessary, roadside attractions of all are gift shops. In their purest manifestations they offer no additional entertainment to travelers, unless, of course, shopping itself is considered a form of amusement. Browsing, admiring, and snickering at knickknacks is certainly a pleasant way to pass the time and to relax, and it gives people a chance to stretch their weary bones, and to use the ever-present sets of restroom facilities.

Perry's Tropical Nut House on Route 1 in East Belfast, Maine, is a roadside stand that evolved into a classic roadside institution. Irving S. Perry, who had owned a cigar factory and then a grocery store in the area, decided in 1926 to import a bunch of pecans from that year's bumper crop and sell them from a stand in front of his house. Mr. Perry, an inveterate collector, added a few curios and museum pieces he had picked up during his travels. After moving to a larger location, Perry, the showman and promoter, transformed his nut house into a house of wonders. He started a nut collection, which he put on display of course, and proceeded to fill his yard with huge carved wood statues, including the famous Perry's elephant. Then he branched out into selling wild strawberry jam, fudge, handwoven baskets, and scented pine pillows.

Today, the third set of owners, Jonathan and Diana Bailey, have enlarged the operation even more, adding a salvaged collection of mounted animals to make an Animal Museum upstairs, and they replaced Old Hawthorne, the full-sized wooden elephant, which had succumbed to the elements, with a new one, Polly Esther. Perry's Tropical Nut House continues to this day as a not-to-be-missed Down East institution, every bit as outrageous and popular today, if not more so, as it was seventy years ago.

The Covered Wagon gift shop on the Lincoln Highway (U.S. Route 30), three miles west of Kearney, Nebraska, is a perfect symbol of roadside exploration on the breathtakingly beautiful plains of the far Midwest. It is a place where time has stood still. The building itself, full of pioneer spirit (the building's location is said to be precisely halfway between Boston and San Francisco), is shaped like a covered wagon with a canvas top and wooden wheels, and it is pulled by two concrete oxen heading west, but going nowhere quickly.

In 1960, old Highway 30 was bypassed once and for all by Interstate 80, and in 1963 the business was sold to its present owners, Nick and Rose Ponticello. Not very many customers come by anymore, and the gift shop is still stuffed with vintage merchandise from the pre-interstate days—souvenir handkerchiefs, felt pennants, moccasins, travel decals, and old linen-textured postcards. Nick and Rose Ponticello, now in their late seventies and married for nearly fifty years, are semi-retired, but they are the very proud proprietors of this highway artifact, the likes of which are seldom to be found anywhere anymore.

While the Covered Wagon is a remnant of days gone by, an attraction called Buffet Flat (also known as the Funny Farm) in Bend, Oregon, is positively New Age. Instead of old Nick and Rose, surprised tourists get to meet two wild and crazy guys named Mike Craven and Gene Corsey. It is an antiques shop gone amok, and their literature speaks for itself: "Is there an empty spot in your life? Does a little love, a dose of pure admiration and some unbridled greed thrown in for spice appeal to you?

. . . Feel your jaw drop when you see the doll house with a TV that really works. Put a new spin on your life at The Agitator Wall. Stroll through the largest Bowling Ball Garden in the Western United States (Yes, Virginia, you can buy the seeds at Buffet Flat). . . . There's all this and Goat Races, and Lucy in the Sky With Diamonds, Pot Bellied Pigs, the Bear, The Cat Habitat, and a whole lot more!"

The places selling produce and other food gifts are perhaps the most tempting businesses of all. Many of them were buildings shaped like what they were offering, making them very hard to miss. A huge chain like Stuckey's relied upon repetition of their graphic symbol to establish its roadside identity, and one's life would not be complete without having experienced a pecan log or a praline from a Stuckey's located along nearly every well-traveled road.

THE OLD WOMAN WHO LIVED IN A SHOE

Opposite top: The Covered Wagon in Kearney, Nebraska, was built on U.S. Highway 30 in 1932 as a gift shop at a point said to be halfway between San Francisco and Boston. This roadside artifact, bypassed long ago by the interstate, was still stocked with vintage souvenirs in 1996.

Opposite, bottom left: Perry's Nut House is a grand and venerable Down East institution along Route 1 in Belfast, Maine. It began in 1926 as a nut stand, and then evolved into much more. Its second owner permanently based a size 144 shoe statue out front which used to be displayed at country fairs.

Opposite, bottom right: Stuckey's began as a lean-to pecan stand in Eastman, Georgia, in 1934. The operation grew and expanded to a chain of some 360 stores, including the one seen here located near Jasper, Tennessee—most stores proclaimed by a series of insistent billboards.

Above right: Buffet Flat is a New Age gift shop and roadside attraction in Bend, Oregon, seen here in 1987 in its former quarters. It was later forced to move across the street when Highway 97 was widened. In its new venue, Buffet Flat has become larger and wackier than ever (below right), and its owners have tried to encourage others to grow their own bowling ball garden by offering packets of bowling ball seeds for sale (below).

BOWLING BALL

GLORIOSA STRIKE-A-BUNDA

$1.00

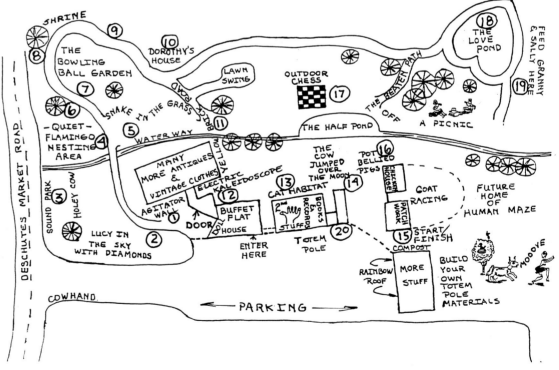

Gift and souvenir shops attached as one element in larger attractions are the common thread linking nearly all roadside spots, and these provide a vital source of additional profits. At the end points of visitors' tours are the places crammed with not only place-specific items, but also a wide and often predictable variety of other merchandise.

Roadside gift shops and curio stores, which exist and thrive on the razor's edge separating folly from necessity, continue to draw throngs of people. In this age of the huge corporate monoliths, computers, and the internet, it is comforting to know that there is still a place left in our civilization for whimsical and ephemeral experiences at roadside.

Left top: The Apache Canyon Trading Post in White City, New Mexico, is situated just north of Carlsbad Caverns and attracts tourists on their way to the great underground.

Left bottom: A fifteen-foot-high Kachina doll was the roadside lure for the Queeman Indian Trading Post along Route 66 in Elk City, Oklahoma.

Above: The Tepee gift shop along U.S. Highway 20 in Cherry Valley, New York (left), was built in the 1940s, and immortalized in this 1959 painting by Michael Burdzilakowski (right). Its new owners, Dee and Margaret Latella, are proud of their distinctive building, although they wanted to redo the original paint job in 1995.

Right: A large group of Indians, wooden and otherwise, pose in front of the Uptown Trading Post in Wisconsin Dells, Wisconsin.

Right: A souvenir stand along Highway 20 in Massachusetts was photographed in 1941 by photographer John Collier. It utilized the time-tested method of spreading out its merchandise within sight of the road to attract customers

Below: The Vikens Fruit Market in the Rio Grande Valley of Texas proclaimed on its sign one of the major reasons for motorists to stop and buy—to "Remember The Folks Back Home."

Below right: A wide variety of souvenir and food items were being offered for sale at the Razorback Trading Post in Mountain Home, Arkansas, in 1980. Even the building itself was for sale, a sure sign that this old Mom-and-Pop business in rural Arkansas was threatened.

Right: Spikehorn Meyer plays possum in front of a vast array of tourist merchandise in the gift shop at his Bear Den in Harrison, Michigan.

Below: A sprayed rock "volcano" facade with a dinosaur skeleton out front make Joe's International Rock & Gem Shop in Orderville, Utah, very hard to miss, which is, of course, the reason for this exuberant design expression.

SOUVENIRS

After our vacations are over and we return to the routine of our everyday lives, we have a collective need to find a way to remember the joys of our far-flung adventures. Souvenirs are a way of re-creating these special places and events.

The very word *souvenir,* from the French and the Latin, is predicated on the concept of re-membering. There is the self-generated and creat-ive experience of preserving our memories—by photographs, movies, and on videotape. There are also more traditional and old-fashioned ways of recording our memories: collecting "special" rocks; pressing flowers; and writing and assembling travel diaries.

The need to cherish memories is also the basis of multibillion-dollar businesses. According to one source, the United States Travel Data Center, tourists spent some $24 billion on retail items in 1990. The tradition of mass-produced souvenirs in this country goes back at least as far as the nine-teenth century. Souvenir china—plates, soap dishes, cream pitchers, cups and saucers, et cetera—was made, very often by manufacturers in Dresden, Staffordshire, and other European locales. Before and just after World War II, the motto "Made In Japan" could be found on a wide variety of tourist-related merchandise.

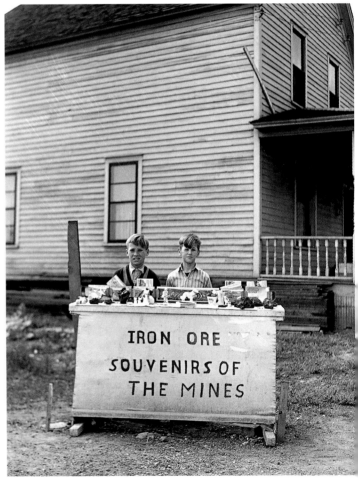

A man selling handcrafted statuary near Bimidji, Minnesota, in 1939, and two boys sell-ing Iron Range artifacts in North Hibbing, Minnesota, in 1941 were captured and enno-bled by Farm Security Administration photographer John Vachon.

Right: If tourists, especially women tourists, couldn't get past Albion L. Clough, the "World's Champion Woman-Hater" in Neddick, Maine, they could buy some of the folk art he was offering for sale beside the road, including a couple of portraits of women.

Below: The Long Horn Museum in Van Buren, Arkansas, was not so much a museum as a roadside stand proffering up horn-crafted items for sale to passersby.

Below right: Jim Frey was nowhere to be seen very early one morning in 1995, in Trenton, Maine, along the commercial strip leading to Mount Desert Island. But Mr. Frey, full of old country trust, had left his splendid birdhouses sitting out overnight at roadside for all to admire and for some to buy.

WORLD'S CHAMPION WOMAN-HATER, THE DREAMER AND HIS BANJO, ALBION L. CLOUGH, CAPE NEDDICK, MAINE

MY OWN MOUNTING WORK HWY 64-71 LONG HORN MUSEUM - NEAR VAN BUREN ARK. HOME OF BOB BURNS

Today, the mass production of souvenirs takes place in odd areas around the globe. They are then imported to the United States to be sold in various gift shop locales. These items, neither unique nor authentic in any way, are standardized products which are then given place identification. The major recent innovation in the souvenir business, dating from the 1960s and 1970s, is "custom-made" tee-shirts and sweatshirts. Whether they are felt pennants, souvenir plates, decals, salt and pepper shakers, ashtrays, or you name it, souvenir items can be found prominently displayed for sale at nearly every tourist attraction in America.

Above: A souvenir plastic fan was sold as a keepsake for the Corn Palace in Mitchell, South Dakota.

Above right: Many of the mainstays of the souvenir business were proclaimed on a sign and sold at the Frontier Fort in Wilmington, North Carolina.

Right: Artist Arto Monaco created a scene of cheerful Christmas bliss as a 1948 tee-shirt design for Santa's Workshop in North Pole, New York, in this pen-and-ink and opaque watercolor rendering.

But not all souvenirs are kitschy junk. There are also handmade objets d'art created by dedicated artists and artisans, and then proffered for sale beside the road. These mementos take on an infinite variety of forms and types—statuary, gadgets, articles of clothing, and even one-of-a-kind birdhouses. Native Americans from various tribes not only produce handcrafted junk dolls with bobbing heads and goofy-faced painted coconuts, they also create exquisite works of jewelry, pottery, blankets and rugs. In the old days of travel, these items could be had for a song; now they command the high prices they deserve.

Top right: A textured, hole-punched hanging plate sold by South of the Border in Dillon, South Carolina, is intended for viewing, not dining.

Right: Wool felt pennants were a popular and inexpensive remembrance of a visit to a tourist attraction, including these for an animal place in Arizona and a Storybook Land in New Jersey.

Whatever their value or significance, it is what these souvenirs symbolize that's important. They are tangible proof of having visited someplace special, and they are a trigger for our recollections. Nearly every one of us has shelled out some money for something with little functional purpose to stoke our memories or to give as gifts to those not fortunate to have come along with us for the ride.

Far right: The saucer of a souvenir demitasse set for the Hot Springs Alligator Farm in Hot Springs, Arkansas, depicted a grouping of its featured reptiles.

Left: A colorful souvenir plate for Santa's Village in Jefferson, New Hampshire, was manufactured by the Adams Potteries, Staffordshire, England.

ELECY

Opposite: The shattered remnants of Mystery Ridge in Au Sable, Michigan, were still a vivid reminder of this tilt-floored attraction in 1988.

Left: A museum and gas station was clinging to life in 1979 along old and bypassed U.S. 10 in McNary, Texas, east of El Paso.

Right: A former peanut store had become the Half Dollar Bar in Peabody, Massachusetts, in 1984.

Overleaf: Arto Monaco's magical castle at the Land of Makebelieve in Upper Jay, New York, stood in high decay in 1996.

Some old tourist attractions not only go away but, sadly, they fade away. Where there were once parking lots full of cars, throngs of people wandering around, and the sounds of excited children filling the air, now there is silence and emptiness. Old buildings, vandalized statues, and faded billboards, overgrown with vegetation, are the melancholy ends of these once joyous and sometimes garish delights. While these old pleasure domes stand deserted and eventually succumb to the forces of neglect and decay, not unlike forests devastated by wildfires, new life arises from the ashes, but usually not at the locus of the devastation. Just as it was at the beginning of auto-

motive tourism in the old days, just around the next corner, several miles away, or even hundreds of miles away, other wonders will appear.

The demand for these so-called unnecessary places will continue unabated. The next generation of tourist attractions will be situated in prime highway locations, near the interstates and at places where tourists now go, and they will present a variety of facilities geared to tourists looking for relaxation, recreation, and fun as they make their own voyages of exploration in the scenic splendor of the United States of America.

ACKNOWLEDGMENTS

THANKS TO: Those people who helped to make this book happen: Terry Hackford, my editor, for her wit and wisdom, and Eric Baker, David Blankenship, and Loreena Persaud, for their excellent book design; Tom Todd for his fine color slides of flat material; Kevin C. Downs, for his superb large-format color transparencies; Paul Haynes and Paul Hogroin at the photo lab at the Library of Congress for their high-quality black-and-white prints of images from the Library's collection; and Mike Mattil, eagle-eyed copyeditor.

Those people who were particularly generous in the sharing of their time, wisdom, research materials, and collections of archival documentation: Arto Monaco, designer extraordinaire of tourist attractions in the Adirondack Mountains of New York State; E. Morgan Williams, who shared his awesome collection of postcards. ephemera, and research; Maureen S. Clark at Clark's Trading Post, North Woodstock, New Hampshire, for her help with the bears; and Jim Heimann for sharing his knowledge and his antique paper collection.

Those organizations and individuals who helped to sponsor and underwrite the cost of the photography and research: The Architectural League of New York; Tom Bailey; Kirk Barneby; Asher Edelman; Rosalie Genevro; the Howard Gilman Foundation; Toni Greenberg; the John Simon Guggenheim Memorial Foundation; Agnes Gund; Ellen Harris; Barbara Jakobson; Philip Johnson; Rick Landau; the Dorothea L. Leonhardt Foundation; the Sydney and Frances Lewis Foundation; Jim McClure; the National Endowment for the Arts in Washington, D.C., a federal agency; the New York Foundation for the Arts; Susan Plum; Joel and Helen Portugal; Harold Ramis; Stephen Resnick; and Bagley and Virginia Wright.

Those individuals and organizations who gave access to their private collections, and those who gave of their time, knowledge, and resources in the preparation of this book: Judy Adams at the Humboldt County Library, Winnemucca, Nevada; Michael J. Baker at the GAF Corporation; William Barry at the Maine Historical Society; Barbara Brackman; Andreas Brown at the Gotham Book Mart, New York City; Ken Brown; Lee Brown; Brian A. Butko; Rosantina S. Calvetti at the Robert L. Warren Studio & Camera Shop, Del Rio, Texas; Jim Cara; Wendy Chitty at Dean Color, Glens Falls, New York; Alicia Clarke at the Sanford Museum (Florida); Carolyn Cole at the Los Angeles Public Library; Dave Cole; Lisa Crafts; Lucinda Daly; Lynda Denton; John and Jean Dunning; David Farmer and Kay Bost at the Degolyer Library; Southern Methodist University; Peggy Engel; Betsy Folwell; Lora Fried at the Mohave County Historical Society, Kingman, Arizona.; Mrs. Elizabeth Gresh, St. Petersburg Public Library (Florida); David Griggs at the Carpinteria Valley Museum of History (California); Mary Hall at the Bedford (Indiana) Public Library; Linda Johnson; Maxwell A. Kerr; David Kloppenborg and Susan Dame at the Boot Hill Museum, Dodge City, Kansas; Kevin Kutz; Mary MacKenzie; Jim Masson; Rich Musante; Bruce Nelson; Hal Ottaway; Joyce Phillips, Santa Claus (Indiana) Chamber of Commerce; Ketrina Poole at the North Lincoln County (Oregon) Historical Museum; Don and Newly Preziosi; Jana Prock at the San Antonio (Texas) Public Library; Maria Reidelbach; Cynthia Elyce Rubin; Joe Ryan; Beth L. Savage at the National Register of Historic Places; T.M Sellers; Karen Shatzkin; Mrs. Frank Shaw; Ann Smith at the Harrison (Michigan) Community Library; Roger Steckler; Carole Steele; Cynthia Van Hazinga; Roger B. White at the Division of Transportation, National Museum of American History, Washington, D.C.; Marly Wyckoff at the Traverse Area District Library, Traverse City, Michigan; and Ken Wynne.

The helpful and friendly people in the attraction and amusement businesses who assisted with the research and contributed visual materials. Special thanks to: Mike Craven and Gene Corsey at Buffet Flat, Bend, Oregon; the Clark family and staff at Clark's Trading Post, North Woodstock, New Hampshire; Nick and Rose Ponticello at The Covered Wagon, Kearney, Nebraska; Sandy Strange and Barbara Hodges at Dinosaur World, Eureka Springs, Arkansas; Marian Bailey at Eclectic Science Productions (I.Q. Zoo), Hot Springs, Arkansas; Lucy and Norm Cork at Lucy's Amusement Park Miniature Golf, Minot, North Dakota; Barry Loughrane and Dot Delany at Marineland Ocean Resort, Marineland, Florida; Barbara Massey at Rock City, Lookout Mountain, Georgia; Bill Puckett at St. Augustine Alligator Farm, St. Augustine, Florida; Paula Werne at Holiday World and Splashin' Safari, Santa Claus, Indiana; Bobbie Wages at the Great Escape Fun Park, Lake George, New York; and Bill Hustead and Gayle Eisenbraum at Wall Drug Store, Wall, South Dakota.

SOURCE CREDITS

All contemporary color photographs, unless otherwise noted, were taken by John Margolies in the years noted in the source list below or in the text illustration captions.

All supplementary visual material is from the author's collection, except as noted.

Endleaves: Souvenir transfer decals, c. 1945-1970: Clark's decal, courtesy Clark's Trading Post; Aqua Park decal, Ken Brown and Lisa Crafts Collection; Monkey Island Decal, Jim Heimann Collection.

Page 1: Dinosaur World, Eureka Springs, Arkansas, 1994.

Page 2: Tyranosaurus Rex, Dinosaur World, Eureka Springs, Arkansas, 1994.

Page 3: Magic Forest, Staff Statue, Lake George, New York, 1996.

Pages 4-5: Giant linen postcard (7" x 11"), Rock City, Lookout Mountain, Georgia, c. 1950.

Page 6: Real photo postcard, c. 1930.

Page 7: 1987.

Page 8: (top) White border postcard, c. 1930; (bottom) real photo postcard, c. 1930, Rich Musante Collection.

Page 9: (clockwise from top) Real photo postcard, photo by Gallup; stamp from back of postcard, c. 1940; 1984.

Page 10: (left) White border postcard, c. 1930; (right) accordion postcard folder view, c. 1950.

Page 11: (top) 1988; (bottom) real photo postcard, c. 1930.

Page 12: (left) Double-fold, giant linen souvenir postcard, c. 1950; (right) line art from Webb's City menu cover, c. 1950.

Page 13: (clockwise from upper left) Courtesy Wall Drug; Courtesy Wall Drug; souvenir decal, c. 1960; postcard, c. 1935.

Page 14: (clockwise from left) Brochure cover, c. 1965; 1988; 1988.

Page 15: (clockwise from top) Linen postcard, Don and Newly Preziosi Collection; courtesy Animal Behavior Enterprises/I Q Zoo; linen postcard, Don and Newly Preziosi Collection.

Page 16: (top) Giant linen postcard (7" x 9"), c. 1950; (bottom) line art from Buckhorn brochure, 1922.

Page 17: (top) Jim Heimann Collection; (bottom) accordion postcard folder view, c. 1950; (bottom) Jim Heimann Collection.

Page 18: Brochure cover, c. 1950.

Pages 18-19: Line art from Wakulla Springs brochure, c. 1955.

Page 19: Real photo postcard, c. 1950, Don and Newly Preziosi Collection.

Page 20: (clockwise from top) Postcard, c. 1950, Don and Newly Preziosi Collection; three-fold brochure, c. 1960; real photo postcard, c. 1960, Don and Newly Preziosi Collection.

Page 21: (clockwise from top) Chromolith postcard, c. 1910-1915, Don and Newly Preziosi Collection; real photo postcard, c. 1930, Bruce Nelson Collection; sepia tone postcard, c. 1940, Don and Newly Preziosi Collection.

Page 22: (left) 1988; (center) 1996.

Pages 22-23: (top) 1989; (bottom) 1991.

Page 23: (clockwise from top) 1990; 1984; 1979; 1980; 1985.

Page 24: (left) 1988; (center, top to bottom) 1991; 1988; 1988; 1988; (right) 1988.

Pages 24-25: 1995.

Page 25: (left below) 1990; (center, top to bottom) 1991; 1988; 1980; (right) 1978.

Page 26: (top) 1988.

Pages 26-27: Real photo postcard, c. 1950, Gotham Book Mart Collection, New York City.

Page 27: (top) 1980; (bottom) comic postcard, c. 1960, Don and Newly Preziosi Collection.

Page 28: (left) Real photo postcard, c. 1950, Don and Newly Preziosi Collection; (right) linen postcard, Gotham Book Mart Collection, New York City.

Page 29: (clockwise from top left) 1988; real photo postcard, The L.L. Cook Company, Courtesy GAF Corporation, E. Morgan Williams Collection; linen postcard, Gotham Book Mart Collection, New York City; 1991; real photo postcard, The L.L. Cook Company, Courtesy GAF Corporation, E. Morgan Williams Collection.

Page 30: Linen postcard, c. 1950.

Page 31: Souvenir photograph, c. 1960.

Page 32: (clockwise from top left) Real photo postcard, c. 1930; souvenir plate, Old English Staffordshire Ware; 1988; 1995; real photo postcard, c. 1950, E. Morgan Williams Collection.

Page 33: (clockwise from top) Real photo postcard, E. Morgan Williams Collection; color linen postcard, c. 1950; color linen postcard, c. 1950.

Page 34: Brochure cover, c. 1955.

Page 35: 1987.

Page 36: (clockwise from top) Photograph by Sussman-Ochs, FPG International; 1987; 1987.

Page 37: Brochure cover, c. 1960.

Page 38: Opaque watercolor drawing by Arto Monaco, 1953, Arto Monaco Collection.

Pages 38-39: Roll of tickets, c. 1975, courtesy Arto Monaco.

Page 39: Photograph by Richard K. Dean, c. 1960.

Page 40: 1996.

Page 41: (clockwise from top left) 1984; 1996; 1996; 1988.

Page 42: 1995

Pages 42-43: Line art from Storyland Cape Cod brochure, Hyannis, Massachusetts, c. 1955.

Page 43: NYSPIX-COMMERCE Photo, courtesy The Great Escape Fun Park.

Page 44: (top) Courtesy Marineland Ocean Resort; (bottom) 1980, Cascade, Colorado.

Page 45: (clockwise from left) 1995; opaque watercolor drawing by Arto Monaco, 1947, Arto Monaco Collection; 1995.

Page 46: (top) Real photo postcard, 1949, Rich Musante Collection; (bottom) 1976.

Pages 46, 47: Line art (decorative border) from 1951 menu at the Christmas Room, Santa Claus Land, Santa Claus, Indiana, 1951, courtesy Holiday World and Splashin' Safari.

Page 47: (left) color linen postcard, c. 1940, Gotham Book Mart Collection, New York City; (right) courtesy Holiday World and Splashin' Safari.

Page 48: (top) 1996; (bottom) courtesy Holiday World and Splasin' Safari.

Page 49: Photograph from UPI/CORBIS-BETTMANN; 1996.

Page 50: Photograph by Richard K. Dean, c. 1960.

Pages 50-51: Brochure cover, c. 1965.

Page 51: (clockwise from top) 1993; 1996; line art from Frontier Town brochure, 1955.

Page 52: (top) Watercolor by Robert Varreyer, 1964, courtesy Great Escape Fun Park; (bottom) photograph by Richard K. Dean, c. 1965.

Page 53: (clockwise from top left) 1988; real photo postcard, photograph by R. L. Warren, courtesy Rosantina S. Calvetti; 1996.

Page 54: (top) Souvenir pillow sham, c. 1960; (bottom) real photo postcard, c. 1950.

Page 55: (top) Souvenir photograph, c. 1925, E. Morgan Williams Collection; (bottom) color linen postcard, c. 1950.

Page 56: Real photo postcard, c. 1950, Don and Newly Preziosi Collection.

Page 57: Real photo postcard, c. 1940; photograph from FPG International.

Page 58: Line art from Musa Isle brochure, Miami, Florida, c. 1950.

Page 59: c. 1960.

Page 60: (top) Chromolith postcard, circa 1915-1920, Jim Heimann Collection; (bottom) real photo postcard, c. 1950.

Page 61: (clockwise from top) Real photo postcard, c. 1950, John ands Jean Dunning Collection; 1985; linen postcard, c. 1950.

Page 62: (top) Chromolith postcard, c. 1910, Jim Heimann Collection; (bottom) postcard, c. 1930.

Page 63: (top) Chromolith postcard, c. 1910; (bottom) real photo postcard, c. 1940.

Page 64: Brochure illustration, c. 1950.

Page 65: (top) Brochure cover, c. 1950; (bottom) courtesy Parrot Jungle and Gardens.

Page 66: Photograph by Frances Robson, c. 1930.

Page 67: (clockwise from top) Real photo postcard, Bruce Nelson Collection; brochure cover, c. 1930; real photo postcard, c. 1930.

Page 68: Real photo postcard, photo by Putnam, courtesy Clark's Trading Post.

Page 69: (clockwise from top left) 1995; souvenir decal, c. 1970; real photo postcard, The L.L. Cook Company, courtesy GAF Corporation, Don and Newly Preziosi Collection.

Page 70: (top) Comic linen postcard, c. 1950; (bottom) 1985.

Page 71: (clockwise from top left) Color linen postcard, c. 1950; booklet cover, Jim Heimann Collection; c. 1960

Page 72: (both) 1990.

Page 73: (clockwise from top) 1990; color linen postcard, c. 1940s; 1990.

Page 74: (both) 1988.

Page 75: (top) 1995; (bottom) line art from brochure cover, c. 1965.

Page 76: (top) Real photo postcard, c. 1930; (bottom) silver border postcard, c. 1930, Cynthia Elyce Rubin Collection

Page 77: (left) Real photo postcard, 1950; (top right) souvenir sticker; (bottom) real photo postcard, c. 1940.

Page 78: Countertop advertising poster, c. 1990, courtesy St. Augustine Alligator Farm.

Page 79: (left) Real photo postcard, Les Esne Studio, E. Morgan Williams Collection; (right) courtesy St. Augustine Alligator Farm.

Page 80: 1980.

Page 81: (top) Keystone View Company, c. 1950, FPG International; (bottom) 1979.

Page 82: 1994.

Page 83: (clockwise from upper left) 1994; 1994; 1987.

Page 84: Real photo postcard, c. 1940, The L.L. Cook Company, courtesy GAF Corporation, E. Morgan Williams Collection.

Page 85: (both) 1988.

Page 86: Color linen postcard, c. 1940s.

Page 87: (clockwise from top left) 1987; 1988; 1991; 1988.

Page 88: Real photo postcard, 1933.

Page 89: 1987.

Page 90: (clockwise from top left) Real photo postcard, 1938; real photo postcard, E. Morgan Williams Collection; hand-tinted real photo postcard, Don and Newly Preziosi Collection.

Page 91: (clockwise from top) Real photo postcard, Don and Newly Preziosi Collection; color linen postcard, Don and Newly Preziosi Collection; Don and Newly Preziosi Collection, 1947.

Page 92: (clockwise from top left) 1987; color linen postcard, c. 1940s; 1987.

Page 93: Real photo postcards, The L.L. Cook Company, courtesy GAF Corporation, E. Morgan Williams Collection (top); Don and Newly Preziosi Collection (bottom).

Page 94: (clockwise from top left) Courtesy Coral Castle; color linen postcard detail; 1990.

Page 95: (clockwise from top left) 1988; color linen postcard, c. 1940s; real photo postcard, c. 1930; 1988.

Page 96: (clockwise from top left) Real photo postcard, E. Morgan Williams Collection; real photo postcard, Jim Heimann Collection; real photo postcard, E. Morgan Williams Collection.

Page 97: (clockwise from top left) Real photo postcard, E. Morgan Williams Collection; smooth linen postcard, E. Morgan Williams Collection; real photo postcard, The L.L. Cook Company, courtesy GAF Corporation, E. Morgan Williams Collection.

Page 98: Valentine, c. 1930.

Page 99: 1985.

Page 100: (left) Security Pacific National Bank Photograph Collection, Los Angeles Public Library; (right) comic postcard, Lee Brown Collection.

Page 101: (top) Maria Reidelbach Collection; (bottom) Security Pacific National Bank Photograph Collection, Los Angeles Public Library.

Page 102: (clockwise from top) Library of Congress; 1988; real photo postcard, photo by Christenson Studio, E. Morgan Williams Collection.

Page 103: (right) comic postcard published by Herbert Hyde, Roger Steckler Collection; (left) Kevin Kutz, 1994.

Page 104: (both) 1988.

Page 105: (clockwise from top right) 1988; 1986; 1988.

Page 106: (clockwise from top right) 1990; 1985; 1987.

Page 107: 1985.

Page 108: Don and Newly Preziosi Collection.

Page 109: 1987.

Page 110: (clockwise from top) 1996; photograph by W.M. Cline Company, Don and Newly Preziosi Collection; 1995.

Page 111: (clockwise from top left) 1987; (both) courtesy Buffet Flat.

Page 112: (top) 1993; (bottom) 1982.

Page 113: (clockwise from top left) 1995; Dee and Margaret Latella Collection; E. Morgan Williams Collection.

Page 114: (bottom) Photograph by John Collier, Farm Security Administration, Library of Congress.

Page 115: (clockwise from top left) The L.L. Cook Company, Courtesy GAF Corporation; 1980; 1987.

Page 116: (both) Library of Congress.

Page 117: (clockwise from top right) Real photo postcard, Cynthia Elyce Rubin Collection; 1995; E. Morgan Williams Collection.

Page 118: (top right) 1985; (bottom right) Arto Monaco Collection.

Page 120: (left) 1979; 1984.

Page 127: Barn billboard, Jesse James Hideout, Route 66, Clyde, Ohio, 1980.

Page 128: Oversize feature matchbook.

BIBLIOGRAPHY

BOOKS

Adams, William R., and Carl Shiver. *The St. Augustine Alligator Farm: A Centennial History.* Southern Heritage Press, 1993.

Andrews, J. J. C. *The Well-Built Elephant and Other Roadside Attractions: A Tribute to American Eccentricity.* Congdon & Weed, 1984.

Ansaldi, Richard. *Souvenirs from the Roadside West.* Harmony Books, 1978.

Ant Farm. *A Trip Down U.S. Highways from World War II to the Future.* E.P. Dutton & Company, 1976.

Baeder, John (text and photographs). *Sign Language: Street Signs as Folk Art.* Harry N. Abrams, Inc., 1996.

Baker, Eric, and Tyler Blik. *Trademarks of the 20's and 30's.* Chronicle Books, 1986.
——. *Trademarks of the 40's and 50's.* Chronicle Books, 1988.

Baker, Eric, and Jane Martin. *Great Inventions, Good Intentions: An Illustrated History of Design Patents.* Chronicle Books, 1990.

Banta, Chris. *Seeing Is Believing?: Haunted Shacks, Mystery Spots, & Other Delightful Phenomena.* Funhouse Press, 1995.

Barth, Jack. *American Quest.* A Fireside Book, Simon & Schuster, 1990.

——. *Roadside Elvis: The Complete State-by-State Travel Guide for Elvis Presley Fans.* Contemporary Books, 1991.

——. *Roadside Hollywood: The Movie Lover's State-by-State Guide to Film Locations, Celebrity Hangouts, Celluloid Tourist Attractions, and More.* Contemporary Books, 1990.

Barth, Jack, Doug Kirby, Ken Smith and Mike Wilkins. *Roadside America.* A Fireside Book, Simon & Schuster, 1986.

Bedeau, Michael A. *Granite Faces and Concrete Critters: Automobile Tourism in the Badlands and Black Hills of South Dakota.* Society For Commercial Archeology, 1994.

Bensen, Arthur L. *The Story of a New York City Tenderfoot and His Adirondack Mountain Adventure.* Frontier Town Productions, n.d.

Beardsley, John. *Gardens of Revelation: Environments by Visionary Artists.* Abbeville Press, 1995.

Black, Carla. *Tiny Town: From Tragedy to Triumph.* Fred Pruett Books, 1990.

Butko, Brian A. *Pennsylvania Traveler's Guide: The Lincoln Highway.* Stackpole Books, 1996.

Dorfles, Gillo. *Kitsch: The World of Bad Taste.* Universe Books, 1969.

Dorson, Richard M. *American Legend: Folklore from the Colonial Period to the Present.* Pantheon Books, 1973.

Dunlap, Beth. *Building a Dream: The Art of Disney Architecture.* Harry N. Abrams, 1996.

Dyer, Rod, and Brad Benedict, text by David Lees. *Coast to Coast: The Best of Travel Decal Art.* Abbeville Press, 1991.

Friedman, Martin (introduction). *Natives and Visionaries* (exhibition catalogue), Walker Art Center, Minneapolis, Minnesota. E .P. Dutton & Company, 1974.

Francaviglia, Richard V. *Main Street Revisited: Time, Space, and Image in Small-Town America.* University of Iowa Press, 1996.

Genovese, Peter. *Roadside New Jersey.* Rutgers University Press, 1994.

Graneman, Eddy. *Monkey Business.* Elmer M. Greening, 1939.

Headley, Gwyn. *Architectural Follies in America.* Preservation Press, John Wiley & Sons, Inc., 1996.

Heimann, Jim, and Rip Georges. *California Crazy: Roadside Vernacular Architecture.* Chronicle Books, 1980.

Hokanson, Drake. *The Lincoln Highway: Main Street Across America.* University of Iowa Press, 1988.

Jakle, John A. *The Tourist: Travel in Twentieth-Century North America.* University of Nebraska Press, 1985.

Jenkins, David B. *Rock City Barns: A Passing Era.* Free Spirit Press, 1997.

Jennings, Dana Close. *Free Ice Water!: The Story of Wall Drug.* Argus Printers, Fourth Printing, 1990.

Jennings, Jan, Editor. *Roadside America: The Automobile in Design and Culture.* Iowa State University Press for the Society for Commercial Archeology, 1990.

Kelly, Susan Croce, and Quinta Scott (Photographic Essay). *Route 66: The Highway and Its People.* University of Oklahoma Press, 1988.

Kirby, Doug, Ken Smith, and Mike Wilkins. *The New Roadside America: The Modern Traveler's Guide to the Wild and Wonderful World of America's Tourist Attractions.* A Fireside Book, Simon & Schuster, 1992.

Knoght, Arthur S. (editor). *Adirondack Guide: Vacationland in Picture, Story and History.* Adirondack Resorts Press, Revised, 1957.

——. *Adirondack and Northway Guide: Vacationland in Picture, Story and History.* Adirondack Resorts Press, Revised, 1963.

Laughead, W.B. (text and illustrations). *The Marvelous Exploits of Paul Bunyan.* The Red River Lumber Company, n.d., c. 1935.

Lawrence County Historical Genealogical Society (compilers). *History of Lawrence County, Indiana, 1818-1995.* Vol. II, Bedford, Indiana.

Leedskalnin, Edward. *A Book in Every Home, Containing Three Subjects: Ed's Sweet Sixteen, Domestic and Political Views.* Edward Leedskalnin, 1936.

Liebs, Chester. *Main Street to Miracle Mile: American Roadside Architecture.* New York Graphic Society/Little, Brown & Company, 1985.

Malcolm, Andrew H., and Roger Strauss III (photographs). *U.S. 1: America's Original Main Street.* St. Martin's Press, 1991.

Margolies, John. *The End of the Road: Vanishing Highway Architecture in America.* Penguin Books in collaboration with the Hudson River Museum, 1977, 1978, 1981.

——. *Home Away From Home: Motels in America.* Bulfinch Press/Little, Brown & Company, 1995.

——. *Pump and Circumstance: Glory Days of the Gas Station.* Bulfinch Press/Little, Brown & Company, 1993.

Margolies, John, Nina Garfinkel, and Maria Reidelbach. *Miniature Golf.* Abbeville Press, 1987.

Margolies, John, and Emily Gwathmey. *Signs of Our Time.* Abbeville Press, 1993.

Marling, Karal Ann. *As Seen on TV: The Visual Culture of Everyday Life in the 1950s.* Harvard University Press, 1994.

——. *The Colossus of Roads: Myth and Symbol Along the American Highway.* University of Minnesota Press, 1984.

Martin, Richard A. *Eternal Spring: Man's 10,000 Years of History at Florida's Silver Springs.* Great Outdoors Press, Second Edition, 1969.

McMurtry, Larry. *Lonesome Dove.* Simon & Schuster, 1985.

Norris, John and Joann. *Amusement Parks: An American Guidebook.* Second Edition. McFarland & Company, Inc., Publishers, 1994.

Paher, Stanley W.. *Nevada Ghost Towns & Mining Camps.* Nevada Publications, n.d., c. 1970.

Patton, Phil. *Open Road: A Celebration of the American Highway.* Simon & Schuster, 1986.

Payton, Leland and Crystal. *Branson: Country Themes and Neon Dreams.* Anderson Publishing, Inc., 1993.

Robbins, Tom. *Another Roadside Attraction.* Doubleday & Company, Inc., 1971.

Rowsome , Jr., Frank. *The Verse by the Side of the Road: The Story of the Burma-Shave Signs and Jingles.* Stephen Greene Press, 1965.

Rubin, Cynthia Elyce, and Morgan Williams. *Larger Than Life: The American Tall-Tale Postcard, 1905-1915.* Abbeville Press, 1990.

Schlereth, Thomas J. *U.S. 40: A Roadscape of the American Experience.* Indiana Historical Society, 1984, 1985.

Sellers, T.M. *Spikehorn: The Life Story of John E. Meyer.* Spikehorn Creek Camp, 1994.

Stefano, Jr., Frank. *Pictorial Souvenirs & Commemoratives of North America.* E.P. Dutton & Company, 1976.

Stern, Jane and Michael. *Amazing America.* David Obst Books, Random House, 1977, 1978.

——. *The Encyclopedia of Bad Taste.* HarperCollins, 1990.

Stern, Jerome, and Gary Monroe (Photographs). *Florida Dreams.* Florida State University Gallery & Museum, 1993.

Stewart, George R., and Erwin Raisz (maps). *U.S. 40: Cross Section of the United States of America.* Riverside Press, Houghton Mifflin Company, 1953.

Stone, Lisa, and Jim Zanzi. *Sacred Spaces and Other Places: A Guide to Grottos and Sculptural Environments in the Upper Midwest.* The School of the Art Institute Press (Chicago), 1993.

Untermeyer, Louis ("Retold by"). *The Wonderful Adventures of Paul Bunyan.* Illustrations by Everett Gee Jackson. Heritage Press, 1945.

Venturi, Robert, Denise Scott Brown, and Steven Izenour. *Learning From Las Vegas.* Revised Edition. MIT Press, 1972.

Wallis, Michael. *Route 66: The Mother Road.* St. Martin's Press, 1990.

Warp, Harold. *A History of Man's Progress from 1830 to the Present.* Harold Warp Pioneer Village Foundation, sixth printing, 1995.

Wilson, John. *Scenic Historic Lookout Mountain.* Chattanooga Free Press, 1977.

Witzel, Michael Karl. *Route 66 Remembered* ("Tourist Traps: Attractions Along the Road," pp. 11-46). Motorbooks International, 1996.

Wood, Frank, and Scott Daymond. *Reflections of Kansas, 1900-1930: A Prairie Postcard Album.* Daywood Publishing Company, 1988.

Yorke, Jr., Douglas A., John Margolies, and Eric Baker. *Hitting The Road: The Art of the American Road Map.* Chronicle Books, 1996.

NATIONAL REGISTER DOCUMENTATION

Evans, E. Raymond, and Vicky Karhu. Lookout Mountain Caverns and Cavern Castle, Chattanooga, Tennessee. Nomination Documentation for the National Register of Historic Places, June 1985.

Gerloff, Scott. Lemmon Petrified Park, Lemmon, South Dakota. Nomination Documentation for the National Register of Historic Places, December 1975.

Primelles, Diana. Marineland, Marineland, Florida. Nomination Documentation for the National Register of Historic Places, March 25, 1986.

Shiver, Carl. St. Augustine Alligator Farm Historic District, St. Augustine, Florida. Nomination Documentation for the National Register of Historic Places, August 3, 1992.

Torma, Carolyn. Dinosaur Park, Rapid City, South Dakota. Nomination Documentation for the National Register of Historic Places, February 28, 1990.

SOUVENIR AND PROMOTIONAL BOOKLETS

Coral Castle: An Engineering Feat Almost Impossible To Believe, 16 pp, 1988.

An Explanation of The Grotto of the Redemption, 28 pp., n.d.

The History of Ruby Falls, 12 pp, c. 1995.

Marineland of Florida: 1938-1988, 28 pp., 1988.

Reptile Gardens: The First 50 Years, 26 pp., 1987.

Roadside America, Shartlesville, Pa., 24 pp., n.d.

See Rock City, two bound-in postcards, 24 pp., ca. 1995.

PERIODICALS

Adirondack Life. "Wish you were here: Hand-tinted memories from Standard Supply," by Elizabeth Folwell, December 1989, pp. 60-63.
——. "Arto Monaco and the company he keeps. . . ," by Peggy Byrne, Fall 1991, pp. 36-39.
American Psychologist. "A Field Of Applied Animal Psychology" [I. Q. Zoo], by Keller and Marian Breland, June 1951, pp. 202-204.
Americana. "Tiny Town's Big Comeback," by Carla F. Black, August 1989, pp. 28 to 33.
Arts + Architecture. Miniature Golf by Allistair Gordon, Volume 2, Number 4, 1884, pp. 73-77.

Atlanta Journal-Atlanta Constitution. "Wacky World: When It Comes to Miniature Golf, Myrtle Beach Is the Goofiest Place on the Planet," by Jim Auchmutey, July 21, 1991, Section M, pp. 1 and 6.
American News, Special Supplement [Aberdeen, South Dakota]. "Storybook Land: 'Where Stories Come Alive,'" May 15, 1996, 12 pp.
Arizona Highways. "Santa Claus" [Arizona], by Orman I. Sprungman, November-December 1943.
Barr's Post Card News. "North Pole: Santa Land, U.S.A.," by Carole Steele, December 14, 1992, pp. 1 and 47.
——. "Father Dobberstein: The Grotto of the Redemption," by Jack Matrow, November 22, 1993, pp. 1 and 44.
——. "One Man's Vision: The Grotto at Dickeyville, Wisconsin," by Barbara Anderson, October 10, 1994, pp. 1 and 47.
——. "Village Museum: Pioneer Village," by Jack Matrow, March 4, 1996, pp. 1 and 43.
——. "Clock Carvers: The Bily Brothers of Spillville, Iowa," by Barbara L. Anderson, April 14, 1997, pp. 1 and 44.
——. "Greatest Pleasures: Summer Vacation," by Bob Fesler, May 26, 1997, pp. 1 and 34.
Berkshire. "Along The Mohawk Trail," by Linda Kinsey, Autumn 1995, pp. 28-35.
Chicago Tribune. "Highway signs point the way to a bustling oasis" [Wall Drug], by Rogers Worthington, January 20, 1989, pp. 1-6.
Chattanooga News-Free Press. "Mrs. Frieda M. Carter Dies at Mountain Home; She Dreamed a Dream of Beauty" [Rock City], July 11, 1964.
Chattanooga Times. "John Garnet Carter Dead; Promoter, Built Rock City," September 22, 1954.
——. "Ruby Falls placed on National Register, but tours of the lower cave are shelved," by Bill Dedman, February 26, 1986, pp. C1 & ff.
Collier's. " Small Game Hunters" [Miniature Golf], by Grantland Rice, September 20, 1930, p. 19.
Clarion. "The Midwestern Corn Palaces: A 'Maize' of Detail and Wonder," by Cynthia Elyce Rubin, Fall 1983, pp. 24-31.
Daily News Magazine {New York City]. "Santa Elsewhere," by John Margolies, December 23, 1984, p. 20.
Dayton Daily News. "In loving memory, a tiny city of stone," by Vincent A. Del Guidice, July 8, 1979, p. 1-B.
Games. "Let Us Now Praise Miniature Golf," by Robert Abbott, July/August, 1981, pp. 10-12.
Grand Traverse Herald. "Rebuilding the city" [Miniature Traverse City], by Eric Dick, August 15, 1996.
Humboldt Star and the Silver State. "Dirty Rose Hotel Safe Now in Possession of Dad Lee," January 7, 1932, pp. 1 and 4.
——. "'Dad Lee' Dies Suddenly: King of Desert Stricken at Lee Center Station," March 16, 1934, p. 1.
Inside Track. "Forget that saying about 'too many cooks'...Holiday World celebrates its 50th year of holiday cheer" [Santa Claus Land], by Mark Wyatt, May 1995, pp. 16-17 and 19.

Kingman Daily Mine, Mohave Magazine Supplement. "All About Santa Claus: Santa Claus Ariz., That Is, On Highway 39," by Keith Leighty, December 1976-January 1977, pp. 45 to 46,.
Lake Placid News. "A pioneer in Breeding of Fur Bearing Animals Who Has Helped Win Recognition of Industry [James Sterling, Sterling-Alaska Game Farm], September 8, 1922, p. 12.
——. "J.S. Sterling Dies in Miami Beach," March 20, 1959.
Metropolitan Detroit. "The Art of Extinction" [Dinosaur Gardens, Ossineke, Michigan], by Carolyn Kraus, October 1987, pp. 110, 112-113, and 167.
Mid-Atlantic Country. "Adventures in Souvenirland," by Sara Lowen, October 1993, pp.36-41 and 78-79.
Modern Mechanix and Inventions. "I Learned About Lions," by Charles Gay, July 1933, pp. 40-43, and 123.
Morning News Tribune [Tacoma, Washington]. "Hitching Their Dream to a Wagon" [The Covered Wagon, Kearney, Nebraska], by Bart Ripp, May 31, 1993, pp. A1 & ff.
National Humane Review. "The New Animal Psychology" [I.Q. Zoo], by Keller and Marian Breland, March 1954, pp. 10-12 and 26-27.
New York Times. "Cutting Corners on Road, America Takes a Vacation" [South of the Border], by Edwin McDowell, August 10, 1991.
Newsweek. "In Praise of Grass-roots Art," by John McCormick, May 14, 1984, p. 13.
Postcard Collector. "The Palace of Depression," by Don Preziosi, April 1985, pp. 16 and 18.
——. "The I.Q. Zoo," by Don Preziosi, May, 1986, pp. 26-27.
——. "Miniature Golf on Postcards," by Don Preziosi, November 1987, pp. 20, 24, and 28.
——. "The Paper House," by Don Preziosi, July 1988, pp. 24-25.
——. "Inspired Construction," by Don Preziosi, August 1988, pp. 24-25.
——. "Ave Maria Grotto, Cullman, Alabama," by Tom Range, August, 1994, pp. 11-12.
——. "Food For Thought" [South of the Border], by Jennifer Henderson, September 1994, pp. 32 and 34.
——. "South of the Border, SC," by Tom Range, December 1994, pp. 16-17.
——. "Wild Wheels," by Don Preziosi, March 1995, pp. 20-22.
——. "The Buckhorn Curio Store 'Museum,'" by Don Preziosi, September 1995, pp. 58-59.
Products [Pittsburgh Plate Glass Company]. "Storytown USA: Adirondack Kingdom Proves That Nicest Fairy Tales Are Not In Books," Summer 1965, pp. 16-19.
Reader's Digest. "Keller Breland's Amazing 'I.Q. Zoo,'" by Ira Wolfert, October 1957 (condensed from the *Denver Post,* August 18, 1957).
Route 66 Magazine. "That Wooly Bully Buffalo Ranch," by Thomas Arthur Repp, Summer 1997, pp. 52-54.
St. Louis Post-Dispatch Magazine. "Still Having A Ball: Miniature Golf In The '80s,'" by Martha Baker, Photos by Jerry Naumheilm Jr., September 18, 1988, pp. 8-12.
St. Petersburg Times (Florida). "'Doc' Webb, Masterful Marketer, Dies," by Craig Basse, June 4, 1882. pp. 1-B and 10-B..
San Antonio Business Journal. "Cool Crest doesn't putt around with gimmicky golf hazards," by Janice M. Curtis, November 9, 1987, pp. 1 and 24.
Santa Barbara Magazine. "The Rise and Fall of Santa Claus Lane," by Ted Berkman and Denize Cain, November/December 1987, pp. 80 and 79.

Saturday Evening Post. "Christmas Is Their Business" [Santa's Workshop], by William Chapman White, December 19, 1953, pp. 34-35 and 77-79.

——. "Gaudiest Things That Fly," by Helen Muir, April 1951, pp. 40-41, 169-171, and 173.

Smithsonian. "Niagara souvenirs: one man's love affair with kitsch," by Gary Walther, January 1984, pp. 106-111.

Society for Commercial Archeology Journal. "Programmatic Architecture: An Introduction," by David Gebhard, Spring-Summer 1995, pp. 2-7.

——. "Big Critters in the Upper Midwest," by Mike Bedeau and Jim Wilson, Spring-Summer 1995, pp. 8-10.

——. "Miniature Golf on the Miracle Strip," by Tim Hollis, Fall 1995, pp. 10-13.

——. "Teal Roofs and Pecan Logs: A History of Stuckey's Pecan Shops," by Lisa Raflo and Jeffrey Durbin, Fall 1995, pp. 2-8.

Society for Commercial Archeology News. "Catoosa Landmark Getting A Facelift," by Time Dye and Earl Ma, Spring 1997, p. 2.

Time. "Tom Thumb From Tennessee" [Garnet Carter], July 14, 1930.

——. "I.Q. Zoo," February 28, 1955, p. 54.

——. "American Scene-In South Dakota: Buffalo Burgers at Wall Drug," by Jay Branegan, August 31, 1981, p. 8.

Tourist Court Journal. "How off-beat theme sells rooms & food" [South of the Border], by Joseph C. Dabney, September 1961, pp. 23 & ff.

USA Today. "Expanding under one roof; Some stores branch out by staying put; One-store giants thrive" [Wall Drug], by Constance Mitchell, Money Section, February 26, 1985, pp. 1B-2B..

——. "1,000 acres of kitsch on the road" [South of the Border], by Cathy Lynn Grossman. Life Section, June 29, 1994, pp. 1D-2D.

Wall Street Journal. "Wall, S.D. Has Population of only 800, But Its Drugstore Draws 10,000 A Day," by Richard D. James, September 5, 1973.

——. "Roadside Signs Lure Drivers to 'the Thing' and to Other Things," by Susan Carey, August 19, 1982, pp. 1 and ff.

——. "South of the Border: Things Are Popping This Fourth of July," July 3, 1987.

——. "Concrete Hogs Giving Dogs a Run As Midwest's Choice Lawn Fixture," by Joan Kron, December 26, 1984.

Washburn County Register [Shell Lake, Wisconsin], "McKays continue legacy of Museum of Woodcarving," Second Section, June 17, 1993, p. 5.

Yankee. "Not Too Big for Little Ones" [Story Land, Glen, New Hampshire], by Bob Trebilcock, June 1995, pp. 52 and 54.

In memory of David Gebhard, an architectural historian whose purview included not only great monuments by famous architects, but also modest structures, commercial buildings and signs, and the whole world of roadside America.

First Edition

Some of the illustrations in this book are published with the permission of private collectors, institutions, and corporations who are listed with the source credits beginning on page 123.

ISBN 0-8212-2351-8

Library of Congress Catalog Card Number 97-075127

Bulfinch Press is an imprint and trademark of Little, Brown and Company (Inc.)
Published simultaneously in Canada by Little, Brown & Company (Canada) Limited
Design by Eric Baker Design Associates, Inc.
Printed in China

AQUA PARK

AQUARIUM and DEER PARK

PARK RAPIDS, MINN.

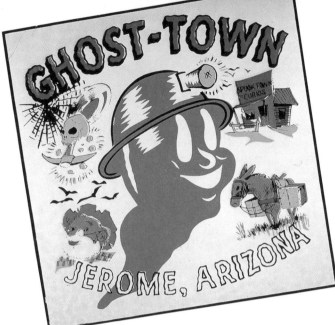

GHOST-TOWN

SPOOK TOWN CURIOS

JEROME, ARIZONA

WE HAD

3300 CAHUEN

HOLLY

WORLD'S LARGEST

ST. AUGUSTINE ALLIGATOR FARM

ROUTE A1A

FLORIDA

1700 N.W. 25TH AVE.

MUSA

HOME OF THE SEMINOLE INDIAN

ISLE

MIAMI

HOME OF THE JACKALOPE

VISIT THE NATURAL BRIDGE

DOUGLAS

WYOMING

SNAKE FARM

LAPLACE, LOUISIANA